Social Indicators for Aboriginal Governance: Insights from the Thamarrurr Region, Northern Territory

J. Taylor

THE AUSTRALIAN NATIONAL UNIVERSITY

E PRESS

Centre for Aboriginal Economic Policy Research
The Australian National University, Canberra

Research Monograph No. 24
2004

ANU

E PRESS

Published by ANU E Press
The Australian National University
Canberra ACT 0200, Australia
Email: anuepress@anu.edu.au
Web: http://epress.anu.edu.au

National Library of Australia
Cataloguing-in-publication entry.

Taylor, John, 1953 -
Social Indicators for Aboriginal Governance: Insights from the Thamarrurr Region,
Northern Territory

ISBN 1 9209421 3 0
ISBN 1 9209421 2 2 (Online document)

1. Aboriginal Australians - Social conditions - Northern Territory - Thamarrurr Region.
2. Aboriginal Australians - Services for - Northern Territory - Thamarrurr Region.
3. Aboriginal Australians - Government policy. I. Australian National University.
Centre for Aboriginal Economic Policy Research. II. Title. (Series : Research
monograph (Australian National University. Centre for Aboriginal Economic Policy
Research) ; no. 24)

994.0049915

Cover design by Brendon McKinley

Contents

Foreword   v
List of figures   vii
List of tables   ix
Abbreviations and acronyms   xi
Acknowledgments   xiii

1. Background and conceptual issues   1

Methods   3
Regional planning   4
What is a region?   5
The Thamarrurr region   9
Baseline profiles   11
Cultural relevance   13

2. Demography of the Thamarrurr region   17

Population size   19
Community census   23
Family size   25
Mobility and service populations   26
Age composition   28
Age grades   31
Population projections   33

3. The regional labour market   39

Regional labour force status   39
Dependency ratios   44
Industry and occupation   45
CDEP activities   50
Estimating future labour force status   52

4. Income from employment and welfare   55

Employment and non-employment income   56
Welfare income   56

5. Education and training   59

Participation in schooling   60
Outcomes   64
Participation in vocational education and training   67

6. Housing and infrastructure   69

Housing   69
Future housing needs   72
Environmental health infrastructure   73

7. Health status   77

Estimation of mortality   77
Cause of death   78
Hospital separations   79
Hospitalisation diagnoses   82
Primary health status   85
Child health   87
Nutrition   88
Health-related quality of life assessment   90
Primary health care services   91

8. Regional involvement in the criminal justice system   93

Data sources   93
Reported offences   94
Correctional services   94
Custodial sentences   95
Juvenile diversion   96

9. Implications for regional planning   97

Demography   97
Jobs and economic status   99
Education and training   100
Housing and infrastructure   101
Health status   101
Criminal justice   102
Information systems for regional planning   103
Partnerships and capacity building   103

References   107

Foreword

Thamarrurr is the cornerstone of our society. It is our way of working together, cooperating with each other, and it is also the basis of our governance system.

In the early days we looked after our families, our clans and our people through Thamarrurr. We arranged ceremonies, marriages, sorted out tribal disputes and many other things. We were people living as a nation. People living our own life.

Suddenly, in the 1930s, white people, traders, prospectors and others came on to people's country. We started to fight back because they were coming on to our land. The government said that we needed help and asked the Church to come in. They brought Western law and a modern way of living.

Thamarrurr then went underground. After that the system never really worked for our people. All of our previous systems of law and governance were replaced. At the time the old people thought it was a good thing. But many were also confused. It was a quiet time a time when we depended on the missionaries. For many years we were directionless. We were told to follow rules and that's it.

But the spirit of the people was still there. Some of our people began to get restless and gradually we starting moving, with the help of many people, to get our governance back. We became more positive and we began to see that this is what we are. Control was reclaimed.

We saw that Thamarrurr gave back people the right to speak for themselves and talk about themselves. We realised that all is equal between people. Even the smallest clans now have a say. We now can stand up and say 'I've got the right to have a say.'

A really big change is happening. We are moving forward. And it will continue.

In many areas, such as the school and other places, we are taking leading roles.

This document is an important tool for our people. At the end of the day we just want to be treated like ordinary Australians. We want our people to have the same living conditions and opportunities as normal Australians. We want our kids to have a chance.

Thanks to everyone, and there are many that participated on this project.

Thamarrurr Region Councillors,
Wadeye
June 2004

List of figures

1.1. Journey to service centres: discrete communities in remote Australia, 1999   7

1.2. Thamarrurr region and ABS geography   10

2.1. Counts and estimates of the Aboriginal population of Port Keats/Wadeye 1950–2001   20

2.2. Distribution of Thamarrurr family groups by size   26

2.3. Settlement distribution in the Thamarrurr region, 2003   28

2.4. Resident Aboriginal population of Thamarrurr Region by age and sex, 2003   29

2.5. Single year sex ratio: resident Aboriginal population of Thamarrurr region, 2003   31

2.6. Projected resident Aboriginal population of Thamarrurr by age and sex, 2023   36

3.1. Labour force status of each age group: Aboriginal residents of the Thamarrurr region, 2001   43

3.2. Distribution of labour force status by age group: Aboriginal residents of the Thamarrurr region, 2001   43

3.3. Distribution of Aboriginal and non-Aboriginal employment by industry division: Thamarrurr region, 2001   46

3.4. Distribution of Aboriginal and non-Aboriginal employment by occupational group: Thamarrurr Region, 2001   47

3.5. CDEP participants by age and sex: Thamarrurr region, August 2003   51

3.6. CDEP participants as a per cent of male and female age groups: Thamarrurr region, August 2003   52

5.1. TRS bilingual instruction distribution, pre-school to Year 7   60

5.2. TRS enrolments, attendance, and attendance rates by school month, 2002 and 2003   61

5.3. Duration of absence from school, TRS 2002   64

6.1. Distribution of environmental health hardware items requiring major repair or replacement: Thamarrurr, 2002   75

7.1. Apparent age-specific hospital patient rates: Aboriginal population of Thamarrurr region, 1998–2002   80

7.2. Apparent age-specific separation rates: Aboriginal population of Thamarrurr region, 1998–2002   81

7.3. Distribution of Thamarrurr region hospital patients by MDC and sex, 1998–2002   84

7.4. Distribution of Thamarrurr region hospital separations by MDC and sex, 1998–2002   85

8.1. Imprisonment rate by age: Wadeye males, 30 June 2002   95

List of tables

1.1. Thamarrurr region: summary of boundary concordances — 10

1.2. Data items secured for the Thamarrurr region from various Commonwealth, Territory, and local agencies — 14

2.1. Aboriginal and non-Aboriginal ABS census counts and post-censal estimates: Thamarrurr region, 2001 — 21

2.2. Summary of population estimates for Thamarrurr region, 2003 — 27

2.3. Resident Aboriginal population of Thamarrurr by five-year age group and sex, 2003 — 30

2.4. Distribution of resident Aboriginal population by select age groups: Thamarrurr region, 2003 — 31

2.5. Murrin-Patha age grades — 32

2.6. Projection of the Aboriginal population of the Thamarrurr Region by five-year age group, 2003–2023 — 35

2.7. Distribution of resident Aboriginal population by select age groups: Thamarrurr region, 2003 — 37

3.1. Labour force status for residents of the Thamarrurr region: 2001 rates — 40

3.2. Implied 2003 levels of labour force status for residents of the Thamarrurr region — 40

3.3. Actual levels and rates of labour force status for Aboriginal residents of the Thamarrurr region, 2003 — 41

3.4. Dependency ratios for the Aboriginal populations of the Thamarrurr region 2003, and the Northern Territory, 2001 — 44

3.5. Aboriginal and non-Aboriginal employment by detailed industry class: Thamarrurr region, 2001 — 48

3.6. Aboriginal and non-Aboriginal employment by detailed occupation unit: Thamarrurr Region, 2001 — 49

3.7. Extra Aboriginal jobs required in the Thamarrurr region by 2023 against selected target employment rates — 53

4.1. Aboriginal and non-Aboriginal annual average personal income by labour force status: Thamarrurr region, 2001 — 56

4.2. Gross annual personal income for Aboriginal and non-Aboriginal adult residents of the Thamarrurr region, 2001 — 57

4.3. Number and amount of Centrelink benefit payments for individuals with a postal address as Wadeye and outstations, 2001 — 57

4.4. Fortnightly and annualised Centrelink payments by type and amount for customers with a postal address as Wadeye and outstations, 2003 — 58

5.1. TRS enrolments and attendance by grade level and sex, September 2003 — 62

5.2. Estimated population-based enrolment and attendance rates by single year of age: TRS, September 2003 — 63

5.3. Highest level of schooling completed among Aboriginal residents of Thamarrurr region, 2003 — 64

5.4. Year 3 and Year 5 MAP performance results for reading: TRS, 1999–2001 — 65

5.5. Year 3 and Year 5 MAP performance results for numeracy: TRS, 1999–2001   66

5.6. Assessable Aboriginal enrolments successfully completed by TAFE course level: Wadeye, 2001   67

6.1. Thamarrurr Regional Council housing stock and Aboriginal service population by location, 2003   70

6.2. Dwellings by bedroom size: Wadeye and outstations, 2003   72

7.1. Aboriginal and non-Aboriginal indirect standardised death rates for the Daly SLA and Northern Territory, 2001   78

7.2. Number of Aboriginal hospital patients and separations: Thamarrurr region residents, 1998–2002   80

7.3. Sex ratios of Aboriginal hospital patients and separations: Thamarrurr region residents, 1998–2002   82

7.4. Distribution of Thamarrurr region hospital patients and separations by MDC and sex, 1998–2002   83

7.5. Notification of chronic diseases by sex: Wadeye clinic, June 2003   86

7.6. Notification of chronic diseases by broad age group: Wadeye clinic, June 2003   87

7.7. Growth assessment of children aged less than five years: Wadeye clinic, 2002   88

7.8. Fresh food category by cost: Wadeye, Darwin and District stores, 2002   90

7.9. Staff by stream and Indigenous status: Wadeye clinic, June 2003   92

8.1. Reported offences by category: Wadeye, 2002   94

Abbreviations and acronyms

ABS Australian Bureau of Statistics

AGPS Australian Government Publishing Service

AHW Aboriginal Health Worker

AIGC Australian Indigenous Geographic Classification

AIAS Australian Institute of Aboriginal Studies (now AIATSIS)

AIATSIS Australian Institute of Aboriginal and Torres Strait Islander Studies

AIHW Australian Institute of Health and Welfare

ANU The Australian National University

ANZSIC Australian and New Zealand Standard Industry Classification

AR-DRG Australian Refined Diagnosis Related Group

ASCO Australian Standard Classification of Occupations

ASFR Age Specific Fertility Rate

ASGC Australian Standard Geographic Classification

ATSIC Aboriginal and Torres Strait Islander Commission

CAEPR Centre for Aboriginal Economic Policy Research

CD Collection District

CDEP Community Development Employment Projects (scheme)

CHINS Community Housing and Infrastructure Needs Survey

CHIP Community Housing Infrastructure Program

COAG Council of Australian Governments

DEST Department of Education, Science and Training

DEWR Department of Employment and Workplace Relations

ERP Estimated Resident Population

GAA Growth Assessment and Action (program)

HIPP Health Infrastructure Priority Projects

IA Indigenous Area

IHANT Indigenous Housing Authority of the Northern Territory

ICCP Indigenous Communities Coordination Pilot

ICD9 International Classification of Diseases, Ninth Revision

IL Indigenous Location

MAP Multiple Assessment Program

MDC Major Diagnostic Category

NAHS National Aboriginal Health Strategy

NATSIS National Aboriginal and Torres Strait Islander Survey

NCEPH National Centre for Epidemiology and Population Health

NHS National Health Survey

NILF Not In the Labour Force

NTDCD Northern Territory Department of Community Development

NTDE Northern Territory Department of Education

NTDEET Northern Territory Department of Employment, Education and Training

NTDHCS Northern Territory Department of Health and Community Services

NTGC Northern Territory Grants Commission

PHCAP Primary Health Care Access Program

QOL Quality Of Life

SLA Statistical Local Area

TAFE Technical and Further Education

TFR Total Fertility Rate

TRBP Thamarrurr Region Business Plan for Community Housing 2002–2006

TRS Thamarrurr Regional School

VET Vocational Education and Training

WHO World Health Organisation

Acknowledgments

This study was commissioned by the partners to the Council of Australian Governments' Indigenous Communities Coordination Pilot trial focused on the Thamarrurr region. Under this arrangement, financial and logistical support was variously provided by the Northern Territory Government, the Commonwealth Department of Family and Community Services, the Australian Bureau of Statistics, and the Thamarrurr Regional Council. As indicated by the latter, numerous people contributed to this project, not least because its support base was the ICCP partnership involving the people of Wadeye and associated communities, as well as Northern Territory and Commonwealth government departments. That the report was compiled at all is one measure of this partnership in progress. As with all such enterprises, though, success is mainly due to the efforts and support of particular individuals and organisations.

First and foremost, I am grateful for the hospitality and interest of the people of Thamarrurr and for the backing and material support of the Thamarrurr Regional Council. In the day-to-day conduct of work in Wadeye and surrounds, I am greatly indebted to Tobias Nganbe, Leon Melpi, Matthias Nemarluk, Timothy Dumoo, Irene Dumoo, Theodora Narndu and the women of the Wadeye Palngun Wurangat, Bernard Jabinee, Gerald Longmair, Francis Madigan, Terry Bullemore, Dale Seaniger, Rain Wenitong, Rick Bliss, Desley Seaniger, Scott McIntyre, Jan Pilcher, Brother Vince, Russell De Jonge, and Bob Tedcastle for their efforts and assistance in the process of data gathering. Bill Ivory of the Northern Territory Department of Community Development also greatly assisted in all stages of the project.

At the Darwin end, special thanks are due to Neil Westbury for his logistical support, while Prue Phillips Brown, Richard Preece, David Coles, Philip May and Diane Smith all provided key inputs

The process of data gathering from Commonwealth and Northern Territory agencies involved numerous individuals, many anonymous, but particular mention should be made of Robyn Elliot, Gayle De La Cruz, Agnese Rinaldi, Nick Scarvelis, Janis Shaw, Ian Pritchard, Stephen Jackson, Jennie Renfree, Bev Fauntleroy, Kate Gumley, Greg Hibble and Xavier Desmarchelier. At the ANU, Kay Dancey assisted by preparing the maps.

Finally, in converting a consultancy report into an ANU E Press publication, I was guided by the comments of two referees and advice from colleagues at the ANU including Jon Altman, Diane Smith, David Martin, Will Sanders, Yohannes Kinfu, Maggie Brady and Frances Morphy. All that aside, the facts and their interpretation as presented remain the sole responsibility of the author

1. Background and conceptual issues

Writing in 1971 on the cusp of change from the assimilationist years of welfare administration to the era of Indigenous self-management, Charles Rowley (1971a: 362–4) described
the myriad mission and government settlements across remote Australia as instrumental
in frustrating urbanisation. In his view, these settlements functioned as 'holding institutions' serving to prevent the inevitable migration of Aboriginal people to towns and
cities (Rowley 1971b: 84). With the benefit of more than 30 years hindsight, during
which time Indigenous people have been free from the institutional and legislative
shackles that governed their place of residence, Rowley's proposition is only partially
upheld. While migration from the bush to towns and cities has undoubtedly occurred,
the overall flow of migration to and from cities has been more or less balanced since the
1970s (Gray 1989; Taylor 2003). Consequently, much of the substantial growth in urban
Indigenous population that has been observed in recent decades simply reflects an increase
in the enumeration of urban-based Indigenous people. That being so, the more striking
and profound observation concerning Indigenous population distribution of the past 30
years (precisely because it does run counter to expectations such as those expressed by
Rowley) concerns the growth in size of remote Aboriginal towns alongside the increased
dispersion of Aboriginal population to outstations on Aboriginal lands. In effect, there
is considerable continuity of non-urban residence despite rising urbanisation (Taylor &
Bell 2004).

Some contemporary opinion would lament this continuity of Indigenous rural settlement
seeking the means to socially engineer migration to urban areas (Reeves 1998; see also
K. Windschuttle, 'Assimilation already a reality', *The Australian*, 1 March 2004). It is
interesting to compare such views with the current activities of Federal, State, and Territory governments which appear increasingly prepared to respond to the reality of a
growing Indigenous population in remote areas by seeking ways to enhance life chances
and life quality *in situ*. Such efforts are in line with a growing search for more efficient
regionalism in Indigenous community governance (Sanders 2004; Smith 2004). This study
takes its cue from these policy directions. It addresses the issue of how and whether
current social and economic conditions in remote regions can be quantified for the purpose
of establishing a baseline against which the impacts of policies designed to improve them
might be subsequently measured. Two recent policy initiatives (one from the Council of
Australian Governments [COAG], and one from the Northern Territory Government)
raise the need for such a question.

As part of its unfolding response to the report of the Council for Aboriginal Reconciliation,
COAG agreed in April 2002 to identify up to 10 communities or regions across Australia
to serve as trial sites for Indigenous Communities Coordination Pilot (ICCP) projects aimed
at effecting whole-of-government cooperative approaches to service delivery with the
aim of enhancing social and economic outcomes. These were to be based on a concept of
'shared responsibility' between the Commonwealth, State and Territory governments,
and communities with the idea of streamlining government processes and supporting

some restoration to local Indigenous populations of responsibility for, and control over, decision-making regarding service delivery and general planning for social and economic development.

Because of long-standing discussions between the Northern Territory government and the population of the Wadeye region to the south-west of Darwin around the issue of restoring a more customary mode of regional governance (Thamarrurr), the Wadeye community accepted a proposal to become one of these trial sites. Accordingly, the newly designated Thamarrurr Regional Council entered into a Shared Responsibility Agreement with the Commonwealth and Northern Territory governments in June 2003. The first stated aim of this agreement was to establish partnerships and share responsibility for achieving *measurable* and sustainable *improvements* for people living in the region. The select emphasis above is to highlight the fundamental role that measurement of improvement was set to play in establishing the efficacy or otherwise of the trial. This has further import as it is also a stated requirement of the regional planning goals set out in the Northern Territory Government's *Stronger Regions Policy* which was announced later in the same year (Northern Territory Government 2003c; Smith 2004) with the ultimate goal of establishing up to 20 new regional authorities across the Territory.

Bureaucratic processes established under both of these policy initiatives will serve to identify mutually determined social, economic, and service delivery outcomes, together with the means to achieve them and assumed responsibilities. Significantly, these are to be codified in a negotiated regional development plan, and then subjected to a regular process of evaluation and monitoring against measurable outcomes. Clearly, for the latter to occur, it is necessary at the outset to establish baseline indicators of social and economic conditions against which any subsequent change can be calibrated. This is what the present study seeks to provide for the Thamarrurr Regional Council area. Such a baseline also generates essential input to the identification of priority development issues and assists in the building of capacity for regional governance by enhancing the flow of information and the degree of local knowledge of social and economic circumstances.

Viewed historically, from a Northern Territory perspective, these policy developments signal a conscious effort to move away from a silo mode of planning and development focused on specific sectors such as Asian trade, growth of the Darwin urban area, pastoral management, the mining sector, and the separate servicing of Aboriginal communities, towards an approach which views Territory development as an integrated whole with the strengths and weaknesses of one region (and community) impacting on all others. It is also an equity and efficiency based model, with needs assessment, equalisation of resource allocation, and measured outcomes as the key drivers. For reasons of spatial distribution and historical exclusion, the implications of the Stronger Regions policy, and the lessons that might emerge from the ICCP Thamarrurr trial, will impact most on the estimated 72 per cent of Aboriginal residents of the Northern Territory who have residential ties to Aboriginal lands (Taylor 2003). It is they who now occupy most of the land area outside of the Territory's urban areas, and it is they who to date have been kept largely outside of formal Territory planning processes.

Partly for this latter reason, the extent to which data of sufficient quantity and quality might exist for the purposes of establishing meaningful baseline profiles for customised areas such as the Thamarrurr region is a moot point. Some indication is available from previous attempts at regional profiling which have been reasonably successful in producing a range of relevant social indicators, though with variability depending on the geographic scale of analysis and on the strength of agency commitment and capacity to generate data from administrative collections (Taylor 1999, 2004; Taylor, Bern & Senior 2000; Taylor & Westbury 2000). What is clear from these efforts, though, is that standard small area statistics as available from the Australian Bureau of Statistics (ABS) in the form of Indigenous community profiles provide only a starting point. Not only do these require 'ground-truthing' in terms of cultural match (Morphy 2002), they are also restricted in scope (and sometimes coverage) and raise the need for additional data to be compiled from alternative sources.

Of course, in regard to the ICCP trials and to the Stronger Regions policy, the measurement of outcomes and provision of associated data is a partnership responsibility involving whole-of-government agencies way beyond the ABS alone. Indeed, compared to previous ad hoc attempts at constructing regional profiles, this notion that all partners to regional agreements have some responsibility to inform the process with available data is innovative. Thus, as the officially sanctioned exercise charged with marshalling baseline information for the Thamarrurr ICCP trial, this study serves as a unique test of the capacity of ICCP partners to produce such data. First, it demonstrates what is currently possible at the regional level. Second, it raises the need for awareness of regional social and economic conditions as an essential input to the identification of priority planning issues. Finally, it outlines key policy implications for regional planning development in the Northern Territory. In particular, with the use of regional population projections, it seeks to shift the emphasis in government and community thinking from one of responding reactively to historic needs, to a more proactive approach based on anticipation of future requirements.

Methods

The task that the ICCP partners have set themselves falls within the disciplinary parameters of regional planning. As an area of public policy and academic endeavour, this is a multifaceted activity and significantly has its roots as a form of applied economics in the United Kingdom of the 1930s where preferential taxation rates and subsidy packages were made available for industries willing to establish themselves in newly proclaimed Special Areas in the more depressed areas of the north and west (McCrone 1969: 93–105). Subsequent regional planning has acquired a firm theoretical basis and assumed far more complex and integrated tasks, being a common tool of government policy (Balchin, Sykora & Bull 1999; Glasson 1983; Gore 1984; Stilwell 1992; Stohr & Fraser Taylor 1981). Its content ranges across the breadth of government functions including the management of environmental, social and economic development, to the point, in some cases, of full regional devolution. The essential point is that regional planning has a long history and has acquired, over the years, a defined literature outlining a set of established conceptual frameworks and analytical techniques.

Of course the ultimate purpose and vehicle for effective regional planning is the strengthening of regional governance, and a key task for policy analysts is to consider what this might mean, how it might be implemented, and above all, to establish the elements that contribute to *good* governance practice (Dodson & Smith 2003). As the background notes to the Northern Territory government's *Building Effective Indigenous Governance* conference pointed out (Northern Territory Government 2003b), 'governance' is not the same as 'government'. 'Government' means having a jurisdictional control, whereas 'governance' is about having the processes and institutional capacity to be able to exercise that control through sound decision-making. Good 'governance', on the other hand, is all about the means to establish this with the ultimate aim of achieving the social, cultural, and economic developments sought by citizens. If this is the aim of good governance, a fundamental question is how do we know when this is accomplished? What information is required to establish this? What data are available to assist in answering these questions? All of these issues are addressed by the establishment of baseline indicators for regional planning.

Regional planning

Regional planning is a sequence of actions designed to solve problems in the future for a specified region (Glasson 1983: 19). Thus, while regional planning problems may vary, in a public policy context they inevitably involve a sequential process that can be conceptualised as a number of logically ordered stages that (interestingly) are discernable in the processes undertaken by Thamarrurr Regional Council and ICCP partners to date:

- demarcation of regional boundaries;
- identification of regional goals;
- formulation of measurable objectives related to goals;
- projection of the future situation;
- generation of alternative courses of action to achieve stated goals and the acceptance of a preferred plan(s);
- evaluation of planned outcomes versus actual outcomes.

Within this schema, Glasson sees a broad distinction between *physical* or *infrastructural* planning (for example, land use, communications, public utilities etc.), and *economic* and *social* planning (for example, job creation, housing development etc), although these are often interrelated and co-dependent (for example, in terms of the relationship that potentially exists between the provision and maintenance of public housing and the formation of a local skilled labour force at Thamarrurr).

Glasson also draws distinction between *allocative* planning and *innovative* or *development* planning. The first of these is concerned with efficiencies and coordination of the regional system. It deals with conflicts over resource allocation, and ensures that processes unfold literally according to plan. Development planning, on the other hand, seeks to change the regional system in ways that are presumed to be for the better. One obvious example would be the pursuit of new industry development in a region, although this raises an immediate question about precisely what is meant by 'development'—an issue that is likely to loom large in the Northern Territory where development planning might include the strengthening of customary economic activity, just as much as it might refer to the enhancement of more mainstream activity (Altman 2002).

Another vital distinction is drawn between planning *goals* and planning *objectives*. Goals are ideals and should be couched in general terms—for example, 'improvement of the living standards and well-being of the regional population' is one that is often stated, and no doubt will be repeatedly so across the COAG ICCP trials and in the course of Northern Territory regional development planning. Objectives, on the other hand, while obviously related to goals, need to be more precisely specified and they should be capable of both attainment and measurement. Their purpose is explicit, rather than implicit—for example, to raise the employment rate in the Thamarrurr region to the Northern Territory average, to reduce the regional housing occupancy rate to an acceptable level, to increase school attendance and enrolment rates, to reduce specific morbidity rates, and so on. While on the surface such objectives appear laudable, and, in theory at least, achievable, the extent to which they are measurable at the regional scale is the more important issue for regional planning and represents the key question for this study. However, before considering measurement issues, the other conceptual foundation of regional planning needs to be considered, namely: What is the region? How is it defined?

What is a region?

The region is a classificatory concept designed to represent physical, cultural, social and economic characteristics for given portions of the earth's surface. The touchstone of regional analysis is diversity—if none were evident, there would be no regions. That regions exist, then, is almost axiomatic. However, there are diverging views as to what they represent and how they should be defined.

The first view of regions considers them to be natural phenomena, as organic entities, representing the spatial manifestation on the earth's surface of long-standing relationships between particular human populations and the lands they occupy. In this scheme, the key defining features of regions are uniformity, coherence, common identity and homogeneity all identified by detailed description of man–land relationships. Such a view provided the basis of much regional analysis (so called regional geography) up to the 1950s where the aim was to identify and map out formal regions based on the spatial identification of internal consistencies and the mutuality of geographic contrasts and distinctions (Freeman 1961; Hartshorne 1939). Peterson's (1976) Aboriginal cultural areas associated with major drainage basins provide the ultimate Australia-wide example. The intellectual roots for this enterprise stemmed from nineteenth-century geographic determinism with the physical environment seen as underpinning the human environment. While now superseded and intellectually marginalised as explanatory of human organisation given the complexities of space in the urban-industrial and globalising world, it may be salutary to reflect on these methodologies when contemplating the design of regional boundaries in the Northern Territory and elsewhere given the continuing import-ance of the land base as an organising feature of Aboriginal social and economic life.

The second, more recent, view sees regions simply as a method of classification—a de-scriptive tool defined according to particular criteria, with as many regions as there are criteria to define them. In this scheme, a particular approach is to identify regions accord-ing to their function, thus distinguishing functional regions from the formal regions mentioned above. A functional region is one that displays a certain functional coher-ence—an interdependence of parts—when defined against certain criteria. They are often described as nodal regions composed of heterogeneous units and populations (typically a network of towns and dependent smaller communities) often identified, or circum-scribed, spatially by the pattern of flows of goods, services and people. The term 'hinter-land' captures this notion well.

In the Northern Territory, for example, the physical separation of people from services generates substantial population mobility. The fact is, despite the predominance of usual residence in small, widely dispersed communities, urban centres loom large in the lives of remote Aboriginal populations. According to one calculation from census data, as much as 10 per cent of Indigenous populations present in regional centres such as Darwin and Alice Springs at any one time, are temporary residents from smaller rural communities (Taylor 1998).

The effect of this mobility to service centres is to create a pool, or catchment, of population around each service town. Some sense of the size of these population catchments, and their spatial extent, was provided for the first time using data from the ABS's 1999 Community Housing and Infrastructure Needs Survey (CHINS) which asked key inform-ants to indicate the nearest town that members of each community usually travel to for banking and major shopping services. In answering this, a total of 35 service centres across the Northern Territory were identified. These ranged in size from large centres, such as Darwin and Alice Springs, to small localities such as Timber Creek and Borroloola. An indication of the spatial pattern of these catchment areas, and therefore of functional regions, is provided in Figure 1.1.

While subjectivity applies to these data due to the nature of the survey methodology based on information sought from key informants, the map clearly illustrates a major functional region centred on Alice Springs and extending across the Western Australian and South Australian borders. In all, 259 communities nominated Alice Springs as their primary source of higher order services, and this encompassed a population of some 15 000. Moving north, other functional regions are evident around Darwin and Katherine, while some parts of the Territory are functionally tied to cross-border towns, as in the case of Kununurra in the East Kimberley region of Western Australia. Wadeye can be seen to form part of Darwin's functional region.

Figure 1.1. Journey to service centres: discrete communities in remote Australia, 1999

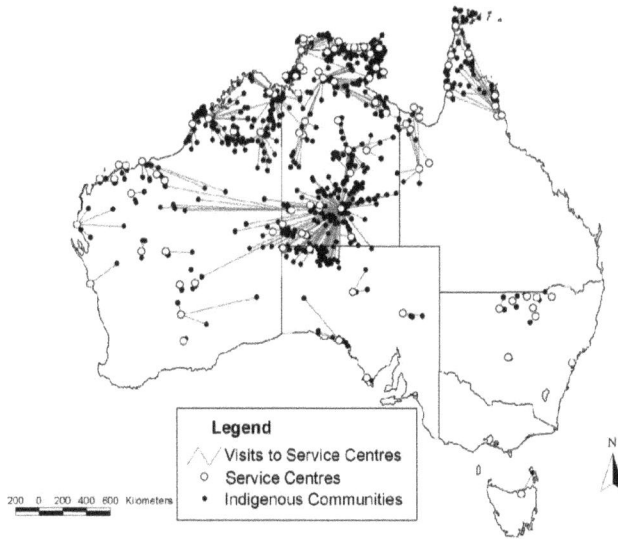

Legend
/\/ Visits to Service Centres
○ Service Centres
• Indigenous Communities

200 0 200 400 600 Kilometers

N

Source: Taylor (2002)

Somewhat intermediary between formal and functional regions is the notion of program-ming, or administrative regions (Stilwell 1992: 46). This provides a more pragmatic view of regions recognising the fact that economic and social institutions tend to operate within administrative boundaries. These represent the boundaries of governance, and for better or worse, invariably provide the framework within which planning decisions are made and services delivered. Within the Australian federal system, State and Territory governments have tended to represent the key intermediary planning level. Perhaps as a consequence of this, planning at the truly regional level has rarely been achieved, with local government and metropolitan jurisdictions acquiring most regional-type functions, although exceptions do exist as in the case of the Kimberley Development Commission and the Murray-Darling Basin Commission with the latter straddling several State boundaries and now encompassing governance arrangements for some 30 Indigenous nations (Taylor & Biddle 2004). In the Northern Territory to date, the five government administrative regions have been established according to an urban centre and hinterland model reflecting (or creating?) functional regions not unlike those identified above.

When it comes to deciding on regional boundaries for new Northern Territory regional bodies, it is likely (if not advisable), that some combination of these regional definitions will be brought to bear, with a possible trade-off between formal cultural regions and the need for economies of scale and recognition of existing service delivery frameworks. This much seems implicit in the Northern Territory Government's definition of a region as:

> an area that the people in it see as a region and that the government agrees should be treated as such; where a reasonable community of in-terest exists; where there is capacity to achieve economies of scale in

the achievement of outcomes; and where there is demonstrated capacity or need for whole of community action to cooperate in the achievement of shared objectives (Northern Territory Government 2003c).

Aside from the Thamarrurr Region, which is already in place, the sorts of regions identified for consideration in this way by the 'Stronger Regions' policy include the Tiwi Islands, Greater Darwin, Kakadu/Coburg, East Arnhem, Groote Eylandt, Maningrida and surrounds, Pine Creek/Coomalie/Douglas-Daly, Katherine, Katherine East (Nyirranggulung), Katherine West, Roper River, Gulf region, Anmatjere, West MacDonnells, Alice Springs, Warlpiri communities and the Tanami, Southern Arrente, Southern Central (Imanpa, Mutitjulu, Kaltukatjara), and Barkly.

While such groupings might appear intuitively sound, complexities are almost certain to arise in seeking to establish boundaries for the purposes of representing regional 'communities of interest' with 'shared objectives'. Some insight into the nature of such complexities for regional planning purposes is available from Sutton's (1995) critique of Davis and Prescott's (1992) work on Aboriginal boundaries, and Morphy's (1999) critique of the Reeves' proposals for reform of the *Aboriginal Land Rights (Northern Territory) Act 1976.*

With reference to the latter, it is pointed out that populations that are now centred around former government settlements and mission stations might appear to provide some basis for regional groupings, but they are unlikely to define traditional levels of regional organisation, which in any case are often indeterminate being blurred at the edges. Even in Eastern Arnhem Land, where a case can be made for a degree of regional coherence based on the kinship system and relatedness of Yolngu languages, people in the western part of the Yolngu region interact with non-Yolngu groups centred in the Maningrida region, while southerly Yolngu groups such as the Ritharrngu have close links with people in Ngukurr and Numbulwar. In both cases, these links are probably closer than the links to the Yolgnu communities at Yirrkala and Galiwinku. According to Morphy (1999: 36), regional differences that seem so clear at a distance often dissolve at the boundaries between regions due to intermarriage and shared ceremonial and economic activity.

While this is no doubt the case, at the end of the day, boundaries for regional planning will need to be established—as, indeed, they already have been for a wide range of service delivery activities including health spending, policing, housing, CDEP, local government distributions, and so on. However, if new regional authorities are to assume an innate sense of regional representation, common purpose and joint planning, as specified in the Stronger Regions policy, it is essential that considerable effort be applied to the careful design of regional boundaries. One important aspect of this is related to the monitoring and evaluation phase of regional planning. At the very least, consideration should be given to matching regional boundaries with the ABS Australian Standard Geographic Classification (ASGC) and Australian Indigenous Geographic Classification (AIGC), as this is the basis upon which official population counts and estimates are developed, for which census data are available, and against which many agencies seek concordance.

However, this is not to preclude the possibility that ABS and agency service delivery boundaries might themselves have to change in order to match new regional planning boundaries. This is not as radical as it might sound. Since 1986, the ABS has successively redesigned Collection District (CD) boundaries to more closely align with socio-spatial groupings on the ground (ABS 1998; Taylor 1992: 171–3), although just how accurate these are in some instances is a matter for debate. It seems highly likely that such realignments might occur again if new regional boundaries suggest the need. In this event, some form of coordination will be essential between relevant Territory government departments, the ABS, and any other relevant agencies such as the Commonwealth Department of Health and Aged Care, and Land Councils. However, as long as the respective boundaries are spatially nested, most of the difficulties presented by any mismatch can be overcome.

The Thamarrurr region

The formal establishment of the Thamarrurr Regional Council can be traced to the collapse of Kardu Numida Council in 1994 and the subsequent search for a more appropriate and sustainable governance structure. This process culminated in a rolling series of Northern Territory government-sponsored workshops and consultations. These were held between January 2002 and March 2003 among Kardu Diminin as traditional landowners of Wadeye, as well as with members of the other 19 clan groups from throughout the region who have variously taken up residence at Wadeye since 1935 on Diminin land. Viewed from a Diminin/Murrin-Patha perspective, these other clan groups include Rak Angileni, Rak Kirnmu, Rak Kubiyirr, Rak Kulingmirr, Rak Kungarlbarl, Rak Kuy, Rak Merrepen, Rak Nardirri, Rak Nemarluk, Rak Nganthawudi, Rak Nuthunthu, Rak Thinti, Rak Perreder, Rak Wudipuli, Yek Diminin, Yek Maninh, Yek Nangu, Yek Ngudanimarn, Yek Wunh, and Yek Yederr.[1]

The purpose of these workshops was to explore and give form to a governance structure that could provide both a legal representation of government functions as required by the contemporary world while reasserting and enabling customary residential rights, albeit in a contemporary form. The term offered to capture this structure, or way of life, was Thamarrurr (Desmarchelier 2001: 4) which described a regional forum that pre-dated European incursion whereby senior people of the different clan groups in the Daly River/Port Keats region would meet periodically to preside over issues of ceremony, use of natural resources, economic transactions and minor law and justice matters (Kardu Numida Incorporated 2002).

Final determination of the regional boundary was made according to instructions obtained via these workshops and it was gazetted on 21 March, 2003 as shown in Figure 1.2. Of interest from the point of view of data collection, is the degree to which this gazetted boundary coincides with other boundaries for which statistical information is available,

---

[1] Use of the term 'clan' is subject to debate among anthropologists. It is used here since it is a term used by Stanner (1936a) to describe Murrin-Patha social organisation and has current legitimacy among Aboriginal people of the Thamarrurr region to describe descent groups with a clear position in the constitution of regional governance.

notably from the ABS and from government agencies concerned with the delivery of services to the region. As Figure 1.2 indicates, the Thamarrurr boundary is almost coincident with the ABS Indigenous Area (IA) for Wadeye and outstations, but it forms only the western corner of the much larger Daly Statistical Local Area (SLA). The degree of match with a range of other administrative boundaries is shown in Table 1.1.

Table 1.1. Thamarrurr region: summary of boundary concordances

Data type	Boundary match
Census counts and characteristics	Almost complete CD/IA match
ABS population estimates	Nested in Daly SLA
PHCAP Health Expenditure Zones	Nested in Top End West Zone
ATSIC CDEP and HIPP/NAHS	Nested in Jabiru Regional Council
NT Education	Nested in Darwin Administrative Zone
NTG Administrative Regions	Nested in Daly sub-region
Police and emergency services	Complete match

Figure 1.2. Thamarrurr region and ABS geography

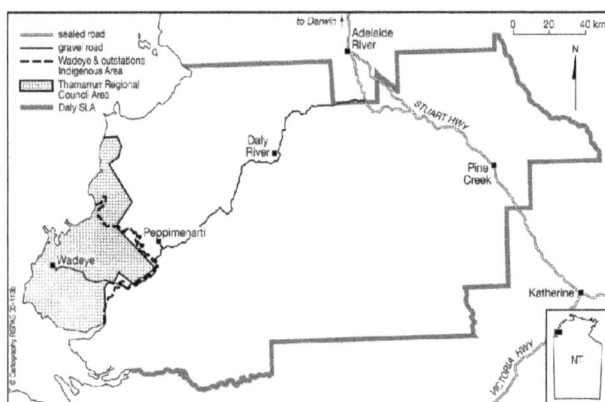

The lack of complete match with ABS CDs (two Thamarrurr outstations fall into a non-Thamarrurr CD) is unfortunate but can be easily rectified with a simple CD redesign. As for official population estimates, because Thamarrurr is nested in the larger Daly SLA, these have to be apportioned to Thamarrurr by ratio allocation to split CDs, although this inevitably involves further reduction in reliability. For this reason, the ABS does not routinely produce such estimates, although it has done so on a consultancy basis for the Northern Territory Department of Health and Community Services. All other boundaries listed cover areas that are substantially wider than the Thamarrurr region, and it is interesting to note that this includes the Commonwealth's Primary Health Care Access Program (PHCAP) Zone boundary as this was reportedly developed following some degree of local consultation and consideration of language and cultural relationships, though with added consideration given to the logistics of existing health service delivery and associated economies of scale (Bartlett et al. 1997: 51).

The tendency, it seems, is that regional boundaries based largely on locally defined cultural criteria (such as Thamarrurr) will produce more, smaller, tightly defined areas, than regional boundaries based on administrative criteria. This was certainly the experience with the evolution of the Aboriginal and Torres Strait Islander Commission (ATSIC) regional council boundaries, which were originally created on the basis of cultural diversity producing 60 regions, though it is interesting to note that these were later reduced to 36 regions due to a declared need for administrative streamlining (Smith 1996).

This lack of boundary match between administrative units and the Thamarrurr Region does not preclude the generation of data for the latter, it simply means that special measures may be required to generate it, whilst care is needed in its interpretation, especially in regard to client data on usual place of residence. For example, administratively, the Kardu Numida Community Development Employment Projects (CDEP) scheme at Wadeye falls under the Jabiru ATSIC Regional Council, yet participant data can be generated separately for the Kardu Numida scheme. At the same time, some of the participants live and work in Palumpa which falls outside the Thamarrurr region and this needs to be both known, and accounted for, when assessing the role of CDEP within the regional employment structure. Likewise, data for clients of the Wadeye clinic can be generated, but not all residents of Thamarrurr are necessarily active clients of Wadeye clinic, with some more likely to be registered at Daly River and elsewhere. The same goes for school enrolments, with some usual residents of Thamarrurr enrolled at school in Palumpa, while high school options are available only in Darwin. Basically, the issue here is that regional boundaries inevitably cut across patterns of service utilisation and administration and this needs to be taken into account when applying administrative data for the purposes of regional profiling.

Baseline profiles

It hardly bears mention that change arising from the COAG trials has the potential to place strain on the social fabric of affected communities, as well as to provide opportunities for betterment. In order to maximise the positives and minimise the negatives, it is central to the implementation of respective agreements that any such consequences of development should be managed rather than arbitrary. A fundamental step in establishing mechanisms for the management of development processes is the construction of a baseline profile of social and economic conditions at the outset. Without this, it is difficult to determine the subsequent effects of one course of action over any other.

The Shared Responsibility Agreement signed in 2003 between the Thamarrurr Regional Council, the Commonwealth, and the Northern Territory Government clearly identifies this need in setting out as its first objective 'the establishment of partnerships for achieving measurable and sustainable improvements for people living in the region'. Two aspects of this key objective have relevance for the present analysis:

- First, it recognises that change must be measurable.
- Second, it acknowledges that measures need to be capable of being established for a regionally defined population.

This requires, as guiding principles, that data items selected for baseline profiling and for subsequent performance measurement and evaluation are replicable over time, and that they are capable of such for the specific population/geographic area selected for the trial.

In responding to this, the approach in the Thamarrurr region was to develop a range of social indicators covering aspects of several key areas of social and economic life that form the basis of policy interest and intervention. Just to elaborate, social indicators are aggregate summary statistics that are strategically selected to reflect the social condition or quality of life of a society or social subgroup. They are typically employed to evaluate the impact of actions taken within a social context for the purpose of producing a particular planning objective.

Thus, determined in part by the development priorities set out within the Thamarrurr Agreement, and dictated also by the availability and replicability of public domain information specific to the Thamarrurr population, the profile presented here covers the demographic structure and residence patterns of the regional population, its labour force status, education and training status, income, welfare, housing and health status, as well as indicators of interaction with the criminal justice system. For each of these categories, the aim is to identify and describe the main characteristics of the Thamarrurr population as at 2003, and to highlight outstanding features and limitations in the data. Also provided are projections of the regional population to 2023 (approximately a generation from now) so as to encourage forward thinking and to anticipate needs and hopefully respond to them before they are realised. This capacity to project future population levels is an essential adjunct to the preparation of baseline data. All too often in Indigenous Affairs, policy has been 'reactive' by responding to historic levels of need thereby creating a constant sense of catch up. What is required if the COAG trials are to be effective catalysts for change is a 'proactive' methodology which seeks to anticipate and plan for expected requirements—essentially a means of translating the content and intent of ICCP agreements into a required quantum of program and partner commitments over a given time frame.

The emphasis placed in the Thamarrurr agreement on evidence-based outcomes underlines the need for accurate demographic data. Whatever the detail of regional plans, it is crucial that these are based on reliable estimates of the population that they are intended for. Globally, this requires reliable totals. Program-wise, it requires reliable breakdown into infants, mothers, school-age children, youth, young adults, middle-aged, and older people. Ideally, it also requires that statistical events in the population (such as employment numbers, school enrolments, hospital separations) are drawn from the same population universe, such that numerators accord with denominators for the calculation of rates. Unfortunately, in constructing regional Indigenous indicators, this is not always certain (Cunningham 1998). That aside, one product of the baseline exercise was the construction of a unit record, demographic database compiled by local working groups and now administered under the umbrella of the Thamarrurr Regional Council as a basic planning tool. This provides a starting point for enhancing the quality of rate calculations as well as for producing data according to family groups, households, and even (as in the Thamarrurr case) clan groups or other socially defined categories in accordance with regional planning goals.

As for other data, an early test of partnership arrangements in the context of baseline profiling was the extent to which Commonwealth, Territory, and local community agencies could, and did, deliver on access to relevant data to support the construction of social indicators as described above. In the Thamarrurr case, the range of data items secured is shown in Table 1.2. An important first step in accessing these data was the bringing together of all relevant Commonwealth and Territory agencies to a common meeting to discuss and negotiate the means by which this would occur. As seen from the data list, the resulting administrative and public domain information is largely restricted to aggregate region-level data.

Cultural relevance

Whatever the availability of data may or may not be, it should be recognised that all sources of social indicator data have drawbacks in terms of providing a meaningful representation of the social and economic status of Aboriginal people in the region. With census data, for example, there are concerns about the cultural relevance of information obtained from an instrument principally designed to establish the characteristics of mainstream Australian life (Smith 1991). Thus, having observed the 2001 Census count first hand at a Northern Territory outstation, Morphy (2002) has described the process of enumeration as a 'collision of systems'. Along with others engaged in the same exercise in Alice Springs (Sanders 2002) and Aurukun (Martin 2002), she concludes that census questions often lack cross-cultural fit and produce answers at times close to nonsensical.

Economic status, for example, would seem to be an unproblematic concept. In mainstream society this is generally measured by indicators such as cash income and levels and ownership of assets. However, among many Aboriginal groups it is often measured in quite different ways. For example, in some tradition-oriented communities, a person's status can be largely determined by access to ritual or religious knowledge rather than to material resources. Similarly, social status can be accrued by controlling the distribution of material resources rather than by being an accumulator (or owner) of resources (Altman 2000: 3–4). In short, materialistic considerations may be of less importance among sections of the Aboriginal population where the emphasis is rather on reciprocity in economic relations (Schwab 1995).

Table 1.2. Data items secured for the Thamarrurr region from various Commonwealth, Territory, and local agencies

Population

ABS census counts and ERPs of Indigenous and non-Indigenous population by five-year age group and sex for Wadeye town and outstations as a group.

Community approval and assistance in conducting a census that distinguishes Indigenous and non-Indigenous populations by single-year age and sex. These data can be manipulated by community working groups into sections of town, individual outstations, and clan groupings.

Clinic estimate of 'active client' Indigenous and non-Indigenous population by five-year age group and sex

Thamarrurr Housing Office population list used to estimate service population

Age and sex of Centrelink customers

Age and sex of regional residents on the electoral roll

Number of Indigenous persons registered with Medicare with a usual address in Thamarrurr

Labour Force

Census data on labour force status, industry, occupation, hours worked, employment and non-employment income by Indigenous status, age and sex

CDEP participants by age, sex, and occupation

Community survey data on individual occupations and skills

Centrelink data

Education and training

School enrolments by age, sex and grade level

School attendance by age, sex and grade level

School Multi Level Assessment Program (MAP) test results for Year 3 and 5 reading and numeracy

Enrolments by training provider category by field of study by certificate level and accreditation category by outcome status by Indigenous status, age and sex

Housing

Housing occupancy rates

Housing stock by occupancy and number of bedrooms

Housing stock by repairs needed

Estimates of housing need

Functionality of environmental health hardware

Health

Chronic disease incidence by age and sex

Growth characteristics of under-fives

Regional food costs compared to elsewhere in NT

Cost of family food basket

Fresh food variety, quality, availability

Unique hospital patients by Major Diagnostic Code (MDC), five year age and sex

Hospital patient separations by MDC by five-year age group and sex

Birth weights

Active client population for clinic by five-year age group and sex

Clinic staffing classification by Indigenous status

Justice

Reported regional property offences and offences against the person

Persons in adult correctional centres by last known address and birthplace (Wadeye)

Juveniles in detention by last known address and birthplace (Wadeye)

Adult conditional liberty caseload according to office (Wadeye)

Juvenile conditional liberty caseload according to office (Wadeye)

Conditional liberty order commencements by office (Wadeye)

Welfare

Centrelink payments by type and number by five-year age group and sex, and $ amount

Non-employment income estimates from the census

Equally, while social indicators report on observable population characteristics, they reveal nothing about more behavioural population attributes such as individual and community priorities and aspirations for enhancing quality of life—indeed the whole question of what this might mean anyway and how it can be measured in an Aboriginal domain has yet to be addressed. Exploratory work on the measurement of community strength in Wadeye provides some initial guidance here (Memmott & Meltzer 2003), while Brady, Kunitz and Nash (1997), and Senior (2003) have explored various notions of well-being in regard to health status. However, none of these provide a universal basis for establishing measurable indicators at this stage. Nor do formal indicators adequately capture the complexity of social arrangements between individuals, families and households. For example, census data identify discrete dwellings as households, but the basic economic and social units of consumption in remote Aboriginal communities are often comprised of linked extended households rather than single ones (Smith 2000). In the Thamarrurr region, there are some 60 extended patrilineal family groups spread across the stock of housing—a key sociological and economic characteristic that is not reported in census data.

2. Demography of the Thamarrurr region

The coastal lowlands to the south-west of Darwin facing the Joseph Bonaparte Gulf are rich in biodiversity based on a range of plant and animal ecosystems which include eroded plateaus, open woodlands, black soil plains, creeks, rivers, flood plains, fringing monsoon forests, coastal mangroves, beaches, and seas. The fact that these lands have high carrying capacity for subsistence living is demonstrated by the existence of six Indigenous languages from three language groups (Walsh 1990) and 20 clan estates within the relatively small area of the Thamarrurr region (approximately 105 km long by 75 km wide). Socially and economically, the area now circumscribed by the Thamarrurr Regional Council has been part of the complex of relatively dense Aboriginal settlement that has existed along the Northern Territory coast since time immemorial with systems of inter-tribal economic exchange connecting coastal peoples from the Darwin region through to the east Kimberley. Significantly, peoples of the Thamarrurr region connect the *wunan* exchange cycle from the south with the *merbok* system to the north (Akerman 1979; Stanner 1933b: 34).

Despite the cultural importance of the region in the Aboriginal world, from a non-Indigenous perspective the area between the Daly and Fitzmaurice rivers was one of the least known parts of the continent up to the mid 1930s (Stanner 1933b: 381). The numbers resident there were simply 'guesstimated' for pre-war censuses and then incorporated into the general estimate of full-blood Aboriginal population for the entire Daly River census district. At the time of first European settlement in the region following the establishment of the Catholic mission in 1935, first at Wentek Nganayi (Old Mission), and then at Port Keats (now Wadeye) in 1939, the Aboriginal population was distributed widely across the region according to custom (Pye 1973). Stanner, who accompanied the missionaries on their arrival at Wentek Nganayi, records that some of those with family and attachments in the region were located as far afield as the pastoral country south of the Fitzmaurice at Bradshaw and Auvergne stations and in the East Kimberley, and more generally around the Daly River farms (Miscellaneous field notebooks 1932–1977, Australian Institute of Aboriginal and Torres Strait Islander Studies [AIATSIS] Stanner Collection Series 4, Item 2).

Stanner's arrival with the missionaries produced the first actual population count. In 1935 he recorded 125 individuals in the vicinity of Wentek Nganayi, and by 1936 he already noted the process of others moving in to congregate around the fledgling mission (Miscellaneous field notebooks 1932–1977, AIATSIS Stanner Collection Series 4, Item 2). Regular annual counting of the population (at least of those in contact with the Port Keats mission) became a requirement in the post-war years as part of the reporting of civil administration, initially to the Native Affairs Branch and then (from 1953) to the Welfare Branch of the Northern Territory Administration. As a consequence, total population counts of Port Keats are available in the Annual Reports of the Northern Territory Administration for each year from 1950 to 1973 and these include the number of male and female adults and children. Subsequently, the official count of the population has been sourced via the five-yearly ABS census. From 1976 to 1996, this provided a count of in-dividuals present at Wadeye on census night, with those at outstations simply included as part of a much larger number representing the balance of the entire Daly SLA. For the 2001 census, however, outstations located in the Thamarrurr region were collectively identified for the first time as an Indigenous Location (IL).

Aside from these counts of the population, various estimates of the resident population have been produced from time to time using a variety of methods and definitions of what constitutes the resident population. For example, the ABS census attempts to count all individuals whose usual residence is at Wadeye IL and Wadeye outstations IL. In recog-nition of the fact that it fails to count some people, the ABS develops post-census estimates of the 'true' resident population by augmenting SLA-level usual residence counts accord-ing to an estimate of those missed (net undercount), as well as other demographic adjust-ments. This produces an Estimated Resident Population (ERP), which in effect becomes the official population of each SLA in Australia for the purposes of electoral representation and financial distributions. As noted in Table 1.1, the Thamarrurr region is nested within the Daly SLA, and so an ERP for Thamarrurr would have to be derived pro rata from the latter. While such adjustment is not routinely carried out by the ABS at sub-SLA level owing to reduced reliability, the ABS did prepare 2001 ERPs for the Indigenous Locations of Wadeye and Wadeye outstations in response to a request from the Northern Territory Department of Health and Community Services. Thus, for 2001, an 'official' ERP for the Thamarrurr region can be said to exist by combining these two.

However, other population estimates are also available. For example, in 1992 and 1999, and then again prior to the 2001 Census, the ABS conducted the CHINS from which it derived an estimate of usual resident numbers for all discrete Aboriginal communities in Australia, no matter how small.[2] As this included all Thamarrurr outstations a complete population estimate for the region can be derived. However, it should be noted that these CHINS data are not based on counts—they represent estimates derived from administrative sources as supplied by key informants, usually council officers. In the case of Thamarrurr, such data would have emanated from the Murin Association, and from the Kardu Numida Council.

In addition to these ABS data, various regional service providers construct population lists of clients drawn from their catchment areas. In Wadeye, for example, the clinic, the school, Centrelink, and the CDEP scheme all service the town population as well as many outlying settlements. Indeed, as a regional centre of some note with employment, housing, banking, retail facilities, and an air route, Wadeye caters for the diverse needs of many individuals throughout the south-west corner of the Territory's Top End, attracting population either on a short-term or long-term basis. Inevitably, such individuals are captured by client listings and these can be variously accessed confidentially to generate

---

[2]Discrete communities are defined by the ABS as geographic locations that are bounded by physical or cadastral boundaries, and inhabited or intended to be inhabited predominantly by Indigenous people (more than 50 per cent), with housing and infrastructure that is either owned or managed on a community basis (ABS 2002b).

useful additional sources of demographic data, if applied judiciously. These are especially helpful in compiling an estimate of service population—usual residents plus short-term residents and visitors who place an added burden on regional services and infrastructure. The Northern Territory Local Government Grants Commission produces such an estimate based on a rolling three-year average of the ERP population and an estimate of visitors. Historically too, a number of attempts have been made by individuals and authorities to derive a population for Wadeye using a mix of head counting and administrative data. For example, in 1982, the clinic reported a population in the region of 1200 (Natoli 1982) while the Northern Territory Department of Community Development (NTDCD) recorded 1156 in 1985 (NTDCD Aboriginal Communities database). In 1994 Desmarchelier (2001: 41) estimated a population of 1950 using a combination of administrative data and head counting. With such a plethora of population counts and estimates based on a variety of methodologies, it is no wonder that some confusion arises as to the precise numbers resident in the Thamarrurr region and exactly which population best represents regional planning needs.

Population size

As noted, initial population numbers in the region remain unknown. However, by 1950 a total of 310 Aboriginal people were counted at Port Keats mission and Stanner claimed in 1952 that the rate of growth was such that the numbers would double within 20 years (*Sydney Morning Herald*, 8 December 1952: 6). According to Long's (1961) survey of the mission population in 1961, this prediction was well on track as he counted 447 residents and noted that others were located at East Arm leprosarium and generally in the 'bush'. By the time of the 1971 Census, the population at Port Keats outstripped Stanner's claim with 766 counted. According to Stanner's assessment (correspondence with Robert Layton, AIATSIS Stanner Collection, Series 4, Item 2) this steady rise in numbers was due to declining death rates and sustained high fertility during the mission years of the 1950s and 1960s, together with some in-migration. The effects of this on population numbers are clearly shown in Figure 2.1. While some post 1971 estimates point to a continuation of this trend of relatively high growth into the self-management era (Natoli (1982) and Desmarchelier (1994) indicating 1200 in 1982 and 1950 in 1994 respectively), the various ABS census counts from 1976 to 2001 suggest a quite different and more subdued trajectory. Between 1971 and 1976, the ABS count at Wadeye barely increased (from 766 to 819). It then fell to 768 in 1981, then rose slightly to 844 in 1986, rose sub-stantially to 1236 in 1991, only to fall again to 1183 in 1996 and to 936 in 2001.

Figure 2.1. Counts and estimates of the Aboriginal population of Port Keats/Wadeye 1950–2001

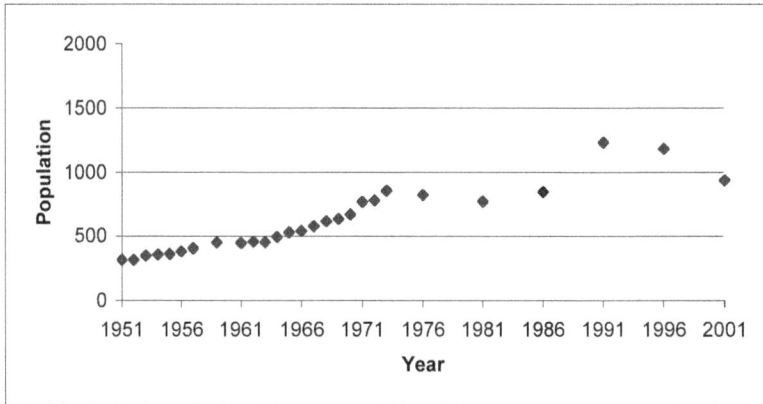

Source: Northern Territory Administration Annual Reports 1951–1969; ABS Census of Population and Housing 1971–2001

These census counts suggest that since 1971 the town of Wadeye experienced a period of no growth, followed by a period of rapid growth, followed by population decline. However, it should be noted that these counts refer only to the settlement at Wadeye and do not include outstations. Up to the 2001 Census, any persons counted at Wadeye outstations were included in the count for the much larger balance of Daly SLA. In 2001, a total of 443 persons were counted within the newly created Wadeye outstations IL. Combined with Wadeye town, this produced a regional total for Thamarrurr of 1379. Unfortunately, as noted, this was the first census that a separate outstation count was recorded and so it is not known to what extent previous census counts for the region might also have been augmented by people present at outstations. Consequently, the regional population trend based on census numbers is difficult to interpret as the Wadeye counts vary widely, and even the number counted at outstations in 2001 (443) appears inexplicably excessive as indications from the 2001 CHINS and from the Murin Association and Thamarrurr Regional Housing Authority (which tend to refer to service populations) are that outstation numbers rarely exceed 150.

Notwithstanding these difficulties, the indication based on historic mission data is that census counts after 1976 fall short of what might have been expected unless one of two demographic events occurred—either a substantial reduction in natural increase, or a significant net out-migration. While evidence to inform these propositions is slim, both Natoli (1982) and Stanley (1985) report an average of 50 plus births per annum at Wadeye in the early 1980s which is suggestive of continued high natural increase in line with that observed during the 1960s. As for the notion that people were leaving the region in large numbers, this does not accord with the corporate recollection of service providers and local leadership. Indeed, one of the factors identified as leading to the collapse of the Kardu Numida Council in 1994 was its inability to respond to the needs of a growing town (Desmarchelier 2001: 41). The only data source that reports on the long-term movement of individuals in and out of the region is the census, and for the most recent inter-census period (1996–2001) this indicates zero net migration for the Indigenous population.

Of course, much depends when comparing population counts and estimates from different sources on the various counting rules applied, as it is rare that these ever match exactly. In respect of the ABS census, it is claimed that each person in Australia is counted only once. At the 2001 Census, this produced a de facto population of 1492 persons for the IA covering Wadeye and outstations (Table 2.1). Of these, 1379 were recorded as Aboriginal persons and 89 as non-Aboriginal. In 24 cases, Aboriginal status was not recorded. These figures were very similar to the numbers recorded as *de jure* usual residents of the same area (Table 2.1).

The ABS uses these *de jure* population counts to produce its final census-based estimates of the population for each SLA in the country. Since Wadeye and its outstations do not comprise an SLA, no official post-census adjustment is available. However, as a consultancy service for the NT Department of Health and Community Services (NTDHCS), the ABS apportioned the 2001 Daly SLA ERP to CD level to derive an 'ERP' for the IA of Wadeye and outstations. This produced a figure of 1665, with the Aboriginal population component amounting to 1552 (Table 2.1).

Table 2.1. Aboriginal and non-Aboriginal ABS census counts and post-censal estimates[a]: Thamarrurr region[b], 2001

	Aboriginal	Non-Aboriginal	Not stated	Total
Census count (de facto)	1379	89	24	1492
Usual residence count (de jure)	1396	94	23	1513
Estimated usual residents (ERP)	1552	113	n/a	1665

a.   The ERP cited in this table was derived by the ABS using a crude methodology and provided to the DHCS Health Zones project. The ABS does not directly prepare sub-SLA ERPs as the data required to support them is not available at this geographic level. The ABS apportions SLA level ERPs to CDs in order to facilitate the estimation of the approximate populations for non-standard regions. However, these do not have the same quality status as directly estimated state and territory level ERPs.

b.   b. Wadeye and outstations IA

Source: ABS Darwin, customised tables

For a number of reasons, doubts were raised by local service providers and community leaders in the Thamarrurr region regarding the utility of this ABS estimate for the purposes of establishing regional planning needs; it was considered to inadequately represent the true size, and to some extent the composition, of the resident population. In support of this belief, a number of alternate estimates of the population were presented, all pointing to the likelihood of higher numbers. While demographic information supplied by

Centrelink in respect of clients with an address in Wadeye did yield a population in line with the ABS estimate that was supplied to the DHCS, this was insufficient to overcome the weight of evidence feeding local perceptions. This evidence included:

- An estimate of Aboriginal usual residents compiled in 1994 based on a head count in combination with local administrative records derived a population of 1950 for Wadeye (Desmarchelier 2001).
- The Wadeye clinic had an estimate of its 'active client' Aboriginal population of 1916 in August 2003. This was the number of Aboriginal people who were recorded on the Wadeye Health Clinic system and had been attended to at the clinic sufficiently recently for both health workers and local staff to believe that the person currently resided in Wadeye and was not recorded on a health clinic system elsewhere.
- Between March and July of 2003, the Commonwealth Electoral Commission toured the region to update the Commonwealth electoral roll and recorded a total of 940 Aboriginal adults (18 years and over) who indicated a usual residence address within Thamarrurr. Using the ABS age structure for Thamarrurr, this would indicate an overall population somewhere in the region of 1900, not unlike that recorded by the clinic.
- The Health Insurance Commission indicated a total of 2089 Aboriginal clients with a residential address within the Thamarrurr region in August 2003.
- Comparison of the 1996 and 2001 ABS ERPs for the Daly SLA indicated an inter-census growth in the Aboriginal population of barely one per cent per annum—only 58 per cent of the Northern Territory Aboriginal average. These data also indicated a reduction in the population aged 0–4 of almost 10 per cent. By contrast, the perception of local leaders and service providers was of a regional population growing at least at the Territory level, if not higher, with a substantial increase in the number of infants due to high fertility.
- The ABS 2001 ERP for Thamarrurr also indicated that only 41 per cent of the population was less than 15 years of age. This was substantially less than the figure of 47 per cent reported for the Aboriginal population of the Territory as a whole, again contrary to local perceptions.
- The Northern Territory Grants Commission (NTGC) reported an estimated population for the region of 2215 in 2001.
- The 2001 CHINS reported the number of usual residents estimated in the Thamarrurr region as 2360.
- Finally, in August 2003, the Thamarrurr Housing Office had a population register of some 2300 individuals who had resided in the region at some time over the previous year.

Thus, the ERP of the ABS/NTDHCS was only one of several population estimates available to the Thamarrurr council for planning purposes, although it is the only one of those listed above that claims to be based on individuals who are uniquely recorded as usual residents of the Thamarrurr region and nowhere else, even though the final number is estimated. The term 'aims to' is used here as individuals are often not physically or individually 'counted' in the census since information regarding individuals is invariably gleaned from a select key informant (or informants) at each household in respect of other household members. This practise of using key informants to glean information about community residents is also used in compiling some of these other estimates.

Obviously, because of the different methodologies applied, the ABS/NTDHCS ERP is not directly comparable to these other figures. If we take the clinic population figure as an example, aside from the different basis for counting (essentially a population list of recent clients assumed not to be on any other list), the clinic figure does not incorporate the whole regional population as it omits infrequent users of the clinic as well as some of those from outlying settlements in the east of the region (such as Nemarluk, Wudapuli, and Merrepen), who are more likely to be serviced by Daly River clinic. It is also the case that some of these other estimates (NTGC, CHINS and the Thamarrurr Housing Office) refer more to a service population level, rather than an estimate of usually resident population. NTGC figures, for example, refer explicitly to an estimate of the populations 'serviced' by councils. To establish these, the Commission receives from councils an annual estimate of the populations that they service based on a variety of methods including head counts, housing records, and environmental health surveys. It then uses public hearings and council visits to test the veracity of the population figures supplied. This is a quite different methodology and conceptual base for estimation than that used to develop ABS ERPs.

In addition to these methodological differences, a further distinction between most of these figures and the ABS/NTDHCS ERP is, of course, the fact that the former refer mostly to 2003, whereas the ABS/NTDHCS figure is for 2001. Thus, to compare at all, even if this were conceptually meaningful, would require the 2001 ERP to be re-estimated for 2003. This is something that ABS methods do not provide for owing to a lack of data to inform sub-SLA inter-census estimates. However, in the absence of a reliable methodology, a crude approximation of this can be calculated using expected natural increase between 2001 and 2003 on the basis of recent levels in the Daly SLA apportioned to Thamarrurr. From this, it can be assumed that an ABS/NTDHCS Indigenous ERP for 2003, were it to be established, would have been around 1700.

Community census

In the realpolitik of community funding and representation, this difference between ABS counts, the ABS/NTDHCS ERP, and other indications of the regional population tends to feed concerns that 'official' ABS data fail to adequately establish the true usual resident population level, with due acknowledgment that this differs from a service population. Accordingly, the Thamarrurr Council expressed a desire to validate its usually resident population as an essential first step in the construction of a socio-economic profile for the region. In discussions with council members and local service providers, it was decided that the only approach suited to this purpose was to conduct a new count of the regional population employing local people as enumerators and advisors. This activity immediately developed as an exercise in community capacity building among the working groups established as part of the ICCP partnership agreement, especially those concerned with housing and construction, family and women, and youth.

By assembling a team of senior men and women via the Thamarrurr Council and the Wadeye Palngun Wurnangat (Wadeye Women's Association) with assistance enlisted via them from representatives of the various clan groups within Wadeye camps and outlying outstations the basic strategy was to conduct a count of individuals present (including absent usual residents) in the region, and to then cross-check this against the Thamarrurr Housing Office population list to identify and follow-up any discrepancies between the two. Interviewers were instructed to include all individuals who considered themselves to be usual residents of Thamarrurr using the same criteria as applied by the ABS (expected residence in Thamarrurr for more than half of the current year). Where individuals were not asked this question directly, the usual residence status of household members was gleaned from the main respondent or key informant. Typically, as with most survey work in remote Aboriginal communities, this information gathering was a communal activity, although unlike the census and other activities such as housing surveys, the information sought was kept to an absolute minimum, with the focus solely on establishing the name, age, and sex of all individuals considered to be usual residents according to the criteria set.

These dwelling counts took place during most of August 2003, although because of limited resources and the myriad of other activities that placed demands on the time of interviewers, direct visits were made to only 125 out of 151 dwellings in Wadeye. For the same reason visits were made to only two outstations (Fossil Head and Nemarluk), with numbers present at the remainder gleaned from relatives in town, and then cross-checked from Housing Office data. Data for the remaining 26 Wadeye dwellings were drawn from Housing Office records and also validated by the survey team.

This initial exercise revealed a population of 1782 individuals for whom Thamarrurr was considered their usual place of residence. The vast majority of these were physically present, whilst some (fewer than 50) were temporarily absent in places such as Palumpa, Peppimenarti, Daly River, Timber Creek, Kununurra, Wyndham and Darwin. Analysis of this initial count by age, sex and location revealed an apparent lack of young children, young men and outstation residents.

Comparison of this initial population count with the Thamarrurr Housing Office population list produced a new list of individuals who appeared on the latter but not on the former. This new list of some 500 individuals was then interrogated by working groups from the Ngepan Patha Centre and the Thamarrurr Housing Office in consultation with representatives from family groups and other agencies, such as the school and the church. The aim was to apply the same residency criteria to these lists. In the process, many duplicates were found, especially among children under 16 years of age owing to their inclusion under both mother's and father's family name. These were deleted. Also found were numerous entries for individuals whose usual place of residence was outside of the Thamarrurr region, particularly in Palumpa, Peppimenarti and Daly River. These were also deleted. A few usual residents who had not been picked up in the dwelling count and who were not found on the new checklist were added, while many of those on the revised list were confirmed as current usual residents, although assigning them to particular dwellings often proved problematic owing to high intra-community mobility. Indeed, one issue for community planning (especially of housing and associated infrastructure), is the difficulty of assigning many individuals to particular dwellings on a fixed basis since the numbers resident at particular dwellings can fluctuate substantially.

Methodologically, this use of population lists to adjudicate on the usual residence status of individuals for those dwellings that were not visited may be seen as diminishing the quality of the final count. However, in the context of high intra-community mobility it may also be seen as beneficial as it reduced the potential for omissions. Certainly, the integrity of community based population lists was established by the fact that the vast majority of those counted were also located on the Thamarrurr Housing Office list. These issues aside, the resulting Aboriginal population amounted to 2034, and this is the figure employed for the purposes of social profiling, unless otherwise stated. Of course, added to this are non-Aboriginal residents. No formal count of these was conducted and so the official estimate of 113 from Table 2.1 is used instead. This produces a total usual resident population for the region of 2147.

Family size

While nuclear family units exist, the functional basis of social organisation in the region is the extended family group and the patrilineal clan (Stanner 1936b: 188). Accordingly, one of the items gathered by the community census was 'family' name, which is patrilineal. From these data, it can be established that presently the Thamarrurr region population (or more precisely, 90% of the population) is organised socially into 60 family groups of 10 persons or more. This is somewhat less than the 78 family groups recorded by Ward (1983), and may suggest that some lines have recently dissipated. The remaining 10 per cent of the population is currently comprised of relatively small social units, made up of either local families whose patrilineal line is diminished, or of assorted individuals and immediate kin whose origins lie outside of the region including places such as Timber Creek, Kununurra, Daly River and Belyuen. These social categories do not necessarily equate with households or the families that occupy particular dwellings, indeed for the most part extended family groups are spread across a number of dwellings within Wadeye and at particular outstations. However, they do provide a starting point from which to classify the population according to locally meaningful social categories since combinations of family groups in the Thamarrurr region broadly cluster into one of 20 patrilineal clan groups (Ward 1983: 3).

Figure 2.2 shows the distribution of extended family groups according to broad size category. There are eight family groups that stand out as large in size with populations of over 50 persons. These include Dumoo, Parmbuck, Cumaiyi, Bunduck, Jongmin, Karui, Mullumbuck and Narjic. Together, they include around 630 individuals. The single largest grouping in terms of collective population numbers (840 persons) are the 28 families of between 20 and 50 persons, although the average family size (17 persons) is found among the 23 families of between 10 and 20 persons. Below this, there are numerous small groupings, sometimes of individuals, with apparently no extended family in the region at least not according to the criteria used here.

Figure 2.2. Distribution of Thamarrurr family groups by size

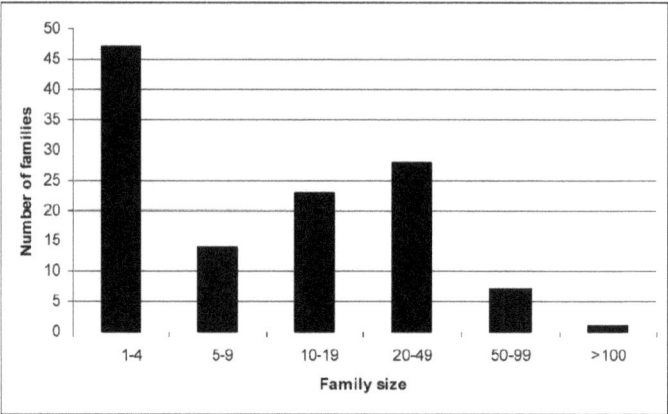

Source: Thamarrurr community census

Mobility and service populations

A service population is literally what it implies—that population which creates a demand for services in a particular location. While this may seem self-evident a number of working definitions exist standard methods for measuring service populations are far from established. The closest to an official line on service populations is provided by the ABS as: 'all persons who access services and facilities generally provided by a local government area. These may be permanent or temporary residents of the area from which the service is sought, or daytime visitors, overnight or short-term visitors to the area' (ABS 1999). This recognises a need for a 'variety of non-resident population definitions which, when combined with ERPs, will be comprehensive of users' service population needs, while singularly will be mutually exclusive of the other component definitions' (ABS 1996b). Clearly, the operational identification of service populations is complex, and the tendency has been to develop relatively simple estimates of visitor numbers to add to usual residents. In the present study, such numbers were derived from the administrative lists of service providers validated by local key informants. The difficulty arises, of course, from the short-term nature of much movement.

In many respects, the identification of an entity called the 'Thamarrurr population' is an entirely artificial construct that cuts across the reality of social and spatial interaction. In addition to those usually resident in the region, there are others (often related kin) from localities adjacent to and well beyond the Thamarrurr boundary who frequently visit and reside in the region while reciprocal visits are also often made. Aboriginal people of the Thamarrurr region have social links that extend over a large area as far north as Belyuen, Darwin and the Tiwi Islands, east to Palumpa, Peppimenarti and Daly River, and south to Timber Creek, Kununurra and Wyndham. Furthermore, considerable short-term circular population movement also occurs within the Thamarrurr region between Wadeye and surrounding outstations, as well as within the town between dwellings. While the bulk of the usual resident population resides continually in Wadeye, daily interaction with outstations is common and the population resident at outlying settlements averages around 150. According to Thamarrurr Housing Office assessment, a seasonal shift occurs with outstation numbers peaking in the dry season (at around 200), and falling by as much as 85 per cent in the wet season when most people reside at Wadeye.

Figure 2.3 shows the distribution of localities within the region. As illustrated, most people live in the town of Wadeye but there are some 20 other localities (all outstations) where families reside either permanently or occasionally. Most of these have some housing and basic infrastructure, while some have none. As the map indicates, these outstations are located either at coastal sites or on slightly elevated ground above flood plains. For the most part, they are located adjacent to environments that are rich in fauna and flora and which provide the basis for customary subsistence-related activities. Aside from the relative lack of housing and basic services, a major factor that restricts more full-time use of these sites is the poor condition of regional roads and bush tracks.

The addition to the overall resident population caused by the temporary residence of individuals and families in the region is estimated using Thamarrurr Housing Office records. These include individuals who were recorded as resident at some time in the Thamarrurr region between August 2002 and August 2003 but who were not considered to be usual residents according to the criteria applied in the community census even though they made use of Thamarrurr services (notably housing). This number totalled 226. If these are added to the 2034 usual residents recorded by the community census, then an overall Aboriginal service population for Thamarrurr in August 2003 of 2260 can be derived. Once again, if non-Aboriginal residents are added to this, then the overall service population of the region is estimated at 2373. This service population figure is the one that should form the basis of funding for major infrastructural requirements. These various population levels are summarised in Table 2.2.

Table 2.2. Summary of population estimates for Thamarrurr region, 2003

Aboriginal usual residents	2034
Total usual residents	2147
Aboriginal service population	2260
Total service population	2373

Source: Community census and Thumarrurr Housing Authority

Figure 2.3. Settlement distribution in the Thamarrurr region, 2003

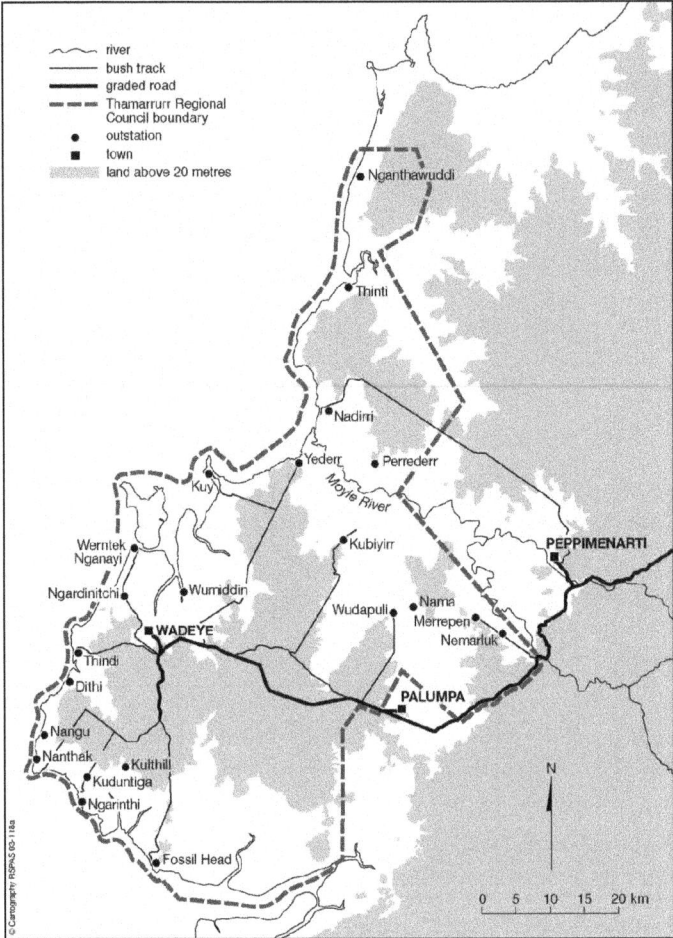

Source: Thamarrurr Regional Council

While temporary residence in the region intermittently adds to the pressure on selected local services (mostly housing), it can also be seen as generating extra demand and enhancing economies of scale for selected service provision. To this extent, temporary residents form an important element of the regional economy and their inclusion in estimates of need, especially for physical infrastructure, is vital.

Age composition

Aside from the overall numbers resident in Thamarrurr, it is the distribution and structure of the population by age and sex that has major implications for social and economic policy development, both in terms of assessing current needs of select target groups, and in determining the future composition of needs as revealed by population projection. The population used here to establish the size of relevant age groups is that obtained by the community census in 2003.

Figure 2.4 shows the shape of the Aboriginal population of Thamarrurr ERP by age and sex. Several features in this age pyramid are worthy of note. First, the broad base and relatively prominent numbers aged 10–14 are suggestive of current high fertility, resurgent after a recent decline, although it may also reflect some age misreporting and possibly undercounting of 5–9-year-olds. Second, the rapid taper with advancing age highlights continued high adult mortality, especially among males. Using the ABS experimental Aboriginal life table for the Northern Territory as a whole, life expectancies for males and females are seemingly stuck at around 56 and 63 years respectively, with much of the excess mortality occurring in adult ages (ABS 2002a). Third, uniformity in the decline of population with age suggests net inter-regional migration balance, although a relative absence of males in the 15–24 age group may well reflect out-migration. Finally, relatively large numbers of women in the childbearing ages, and even larger cohorts beneath them, indicate high potential for future growth in numbers, even if the actual fertility rate were to decline.

Figure 2.4. Resident Aboriginal population of Thamarrurr Region by age and sex, 2003

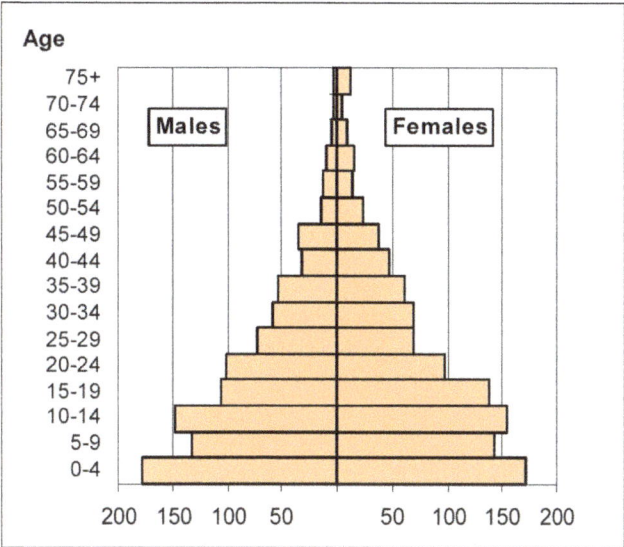

Source: Thamarrurr community census

By contrast, the non-Aboriginal age distribution is typical of a population that is subject to selective migration into the region for the purposes of employment. As much as 85 per cent of non-Aboriginal residents are aged between 15 and 64, with a concentration in the prime working-age group of 25–54 years. While this age pattern is stable over time, it is underpinned by relatively high population turnover with as much as 30 per cent of non-Aboriginal residents indicating that their usual place of residence one year prior to the 2001 Census was outside of the Thamarrurr region. This high level of change in personnel has potentially significant implications for continuity and consistency of approach in key areas of service delivery and administration within the region.

The actual numbers in each five-year age group are provided for the Aboriginal population in Table 2.3. Overall, almost half of the population (45.7%) is less than 15 years of age, with a slightly higher proportion among males (47.7%) compared to females (43.9%), as is to be expected given the observations above regarding differential migration and mortality. Overall the sex ratio of the population is 0.89 which is much lower than that recorded for the Aboriginal population of the Territory as a whole (0.99). Furthermore, the underlying age distribution of males and females is quite distinctive with females tending to predominate at ages above 29 years, as shown in Figure 2.5.

Table 2.3. Resident Aboriginal population of Thamarrurr by five-year age group and sex, 2003

Age (years)	Males		Females		Total	
	No.	%	No.	%	No.	%
0–4	178	18.5	172	16.0	350	17.2
5–9	133	13.8	144	13.4	277	13.6
10–14	148	15.4	155	14.5	303	14.9
15–19	106	11.0	138	12.9	244	12.0
20–24	101	10.5	97	9.0	198	9.7
25–29	73	7.6	70	6.5	143	7.0
30–34	58	6.0	69	6.4	127	6.2
35–39	53	5.5	61	5.7	114	5.6
40–44	31	3.2	47	4.4	78	3.8
45–49	34	3.5	38	3.5	72	3.5
50–54	14	1.5	24	2.2	38	1.9
55–59	12	1.2	14	1.3	26	1.3
60–64	10	1.0	16	1.5	26	1.3
65–69	5	0.5	10	0.9	15	0.7
70–74	3	0.3	5	0.5	8	0.4
75+	3	0.3	12	1.1	15	0.7
Total	962	100.0	1072	100.0	2034	100.0

Source: Thamarrurr community census

The significance of these age data for policy is best revealed by grouping them into age ranges that typically form the target of policy intervention as shown in Table 2.4. For example, compulsory school age in the Northern Territory ranges from six to 15 years inclusive, although here we have used ages 5–15 to incorporate the pre-school year. Accordingly, the infant years leading up to school age include those aged 0–4 inclusive. The transition years from school to work are indicated as 16–24 years, while the prime working age group is identified as ages 25–49. Typically in the Australian workforce, and in International Labour Organisation convention, working age extends to 64 years with those over 65 years representing the aged and pensionable. However, given the evidence for premature ageing in the Aboriginal population in the context of high levels of adult mortality and morbidity (Divarakan-Brown 1985; Earle & Earle 1999), this has been set here at the much earlier age of 50 years.

Figure 2.5. Single year sex ratio: resident Aboriginal population of Thamarrurr region, 2003

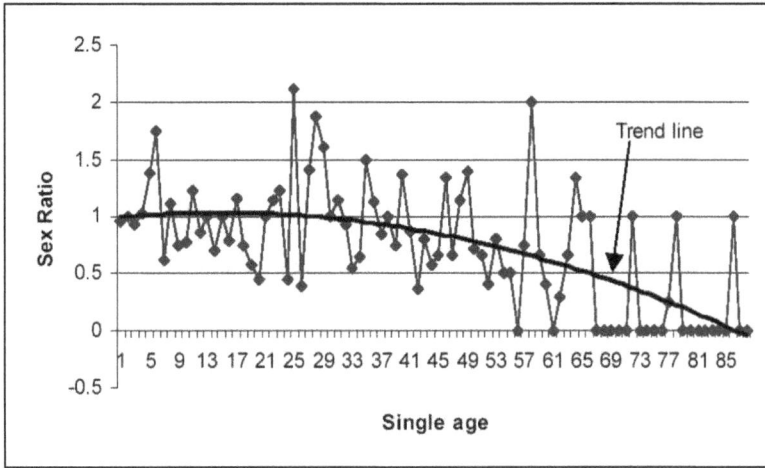

Source: Thamarrurr community census

The results indicate an infant population of some 350 accounting for almost 20 per cent of the regional total, while the school age population of almost 630 is approaching one-third of the regional population. Those in the transition years from school to work number almost 400, or 20 per cent of the population, while the working age group of 530 comprises one-quarter of the total, and is the second largest group after those of school age. By comparison, the relatively small size of the aged population is striking, even given the lower age at which this is set.

Table 2.4. Distribution of resident Aboriginal population by select age groups: Thamarrurr region, 2003

Age (years)	No.			%		
	Males	Females	Total	Males	Females	Total
0-4	178	172	350	18.6	15.9	17.2
5-15	299	327	626	31.3	30.4	30.8
16-24	182	214	396	19.1	19.8	19.5
25-49	249	285	534	26.1	26.4	26.2
50+	47	81	128	4.9	7.5	6.3
Total	955	1079	2034	100.0	100.0	100.0

Source: Thamarrurr community census

Age grades

According to Falkenberg (1962: 176), in Murrin-Patha society of the 1950s, and for all other tribal groups at that time between the Fitzmaurice and Daly Rivers, kinship terms were deployed to express the relative age difference between ego and other individuals, although this was not by reference to actual age but to special age-grade terms. These terms and their cultural significance remain intact. Thus, age grades have important cultural meaning as they express social status and normally indicate whether a person is married or unmarried, initiated or uninitiated, or has a particular degree of prestige and so on (Falkenberg 1962: 184; Stanner 1936a: 311). In such a schema, purely social, ritualised factors have great importance in determining the status of males in particular (cf. Warner 1937: 125–37 discussing status in north-east Arnhem Land societies).

The relevant age-grades in Murrin-Patha society in the 1950s as described by Falkenberg are found in Table 2.5. While the broad progression and underlying social significance remain the same, some of the terms in current usage differ and further work is required to establish these more precisely. For example, *wakul* rather than *konunganga* is now typically used to refer to young children.

Table 2.5. Murrin-Patha age grades

Increasing age	Males	Females
	Konunganga	Konunganga
	Mamai	Madinboi
	Kigai	Nalaru
	Kadu	Palnun
	Kake	Kake
	Nalandar	Kunu'gunu
	Pule[a]	Mutjinga

a.   An additional term (introduced from Western Australia) is used today to indicate a higher ceremonial status beyond Pule. It is often used by senior men but public reference to its name is restricted.

Source: Adapted from Falkenberg (1962: 177)

Returning to Falkenberg's (1962) account, the youngest of the age grades identified (Konunganga) includes all children irrespective of sex up to around the age of about four to six years among boys at which time they are considered Mamai until puberty (Falkenberg 1962: 179–80). Girls, on the other hand, are considered Konunganga through to puberty (Madinboi). In each case, this represents a period of considerable autonomy. Subsequent grades from Mamai through to Kake for men, and Madinboi to Kake for women represent various incremental stages to full adult rights and responsibilities involving several ceremonial rituals for men and marriage and childbearing for women. These broad categories were also recognised by Stanner in 1958 who referred to them as 'age divisions' (AIATSIS Stanner Collection, Field Notes 1932–1981, Series 5, Item 23). In fact he goes much further than Falkenberg in identifying nine stages of childhood (Konunganga) for boys based on physical abilities such as crawling, walking, and running, and then five stages of Mamai with two important ritualised post-Mamai stages (Djauan and Tjambilj) leading into Kigai. Thereafter, three stages precede Kake involving marriage and fatherhood.

Thus, alongside, or woven into contemporary western age categories of infants, pre-schoolers, school age, youth, working age, middle age, old age, and retirement, are uniquely Aboriginal life stages that carry with them different obligations, expectations, behaviours, and statuses. These stages are developmental, ritual and gender-based and often do not mesh neatly with western age categories. For example, the age range from around 10–16 in which western education expects full attendance at school to progress from primary through the years of secondary schooling are also the years when boys progress in stages to manhood with potentially quite different priorities and commitments in mind. Similarly, although working age is conventionally seen in western economic terms as commencing after compulsory school age with the ultimate aim of establishing an independent means to existence, many young Aboriginal men at this age, and for many years beyond, may be viewed as quite junior and lacking in authority depending on their age grade progression, and many young women may already have assumed marriage and motherhood.

While the significance for policy of any mismatch here between the aims of government economic and social policy and the ritualised place of individuals within local society remains to be established, there seems little doubt that the system of age grading was disrupted by the mission practice of establishing dormitories for school age children (Falkenberg & Falkenberg 1981: 34). In recent times the more compulsory nature of schooling and associated restructuring of the regional economy in pursuit of paid employment with their greater emphasis on western knowledge systems may also have unsettled inter-generational relations by introducing positions of authority and status outside of those defined and ritualised by custom. Not surprisingly, then, one of the underlying governance issues expressed by Thamarrurr leaders in seeking to enhance well-being in the region is to ensure that the customary order remains robust (Ivory 2003: 67-70).

Population projections

To date, planning processes in Aboriginal communities have all too often made use of dated demographic information. This creates a sense of uncertainty in assessing the adequacy of policy to address shortfalls in social and economic infrastructure. Such policy development is typically reactive to needs when revealed (for example, in terms of *post facto* responses to housing shortages), as opposed to being proactive by anticipating and planning for expected requirements. However, being proactive requires a measure of future requirements for government works and services, and this is something that is only rarely achieved for Aboriginal communities. This is not the case for mainstream communities throughout Australia where the approach to settlement planning is much more prospective (Bell 1992). For these purposes a standard cohort-component methodology is generally applied, and this practice is adopted here to project the Aboriginal population of Thamarrurr 20 years hence, roughly a generation from now.

Projection assumptions

The cohort-component method carries forward the 2003 population to 2023 by successive five-year periods. The projection is based simply on ageing the population by five-year blocs, subjecting each group to age- and sex-specific mortality, fertility and net migration regimes as follows:

- Survival rates from the Aboriginal life tables for the Northern Territory (ABS 2002b) are applied and held constant for the projection period. This latter assumption is consistent with evidence that life expectancy generally for Aboriginal people in recent times has shown no sign of improvement (Kinfu & Taylor 2002).
- Age specific fertility rates based on registered births as provided by the ABS are not available for Thamarrurr, only for the Daly SLA. While some attempt can be made to distribute these pro rata, this is less than satisfactory. However, one by-product of the Catholic church's continued presence in Wadeye is their interest in maintaining a register of births. In 2001, this reported a total of 76 births to locally resident Aboriginal women. Using the age distribution of mothers for the Daly SLA as a guide, these 76 births were distributed by age of mother and used to calculate Age Specific Fertility Rates (ASFRs). This produced a Total Fertility Rate (TFR) of 4.4, which is very high and substantially higher than the Aboriginal TFR of 2.9 reported by the ABS for the Northern Territory as a whole (ABS 2002b), although it is in line with other relatively high rates reported from similar remote regions of northern Australia (Taylor 2003; Taylor & Bell 2002). It is also interesting to note that even higher fertility (TFR of 9.0) was estimated for Aboriginal women of the Daly River region at the turn of the century suggesting a high fertility norm for the region at the time of European contact (Gray 1983).
- In the absence of an operational model of migration, and in light of the lack of net inter-regional movement reported in the 2001 census, net migration is held at zero for all ages.
- No allowance is made for population change via shifts in Aboriginal identification.

Projection results

The actual projection is conducted separately for males and females in five-year blocs from 2003 to 2023. Projected births for the 2003–2008 period are added to the existing 2003 population and each cohort is then subjected to respective survival rates to arrive at an estimate of the population in each age group in 2008. This process is continued through to 2023.

As for projections of the non-Aboriginal population, these are more problematic since they are driven by economic, rather than demographic, factors. Essentially, non-Aboriginal people reside in the region for the purpose of employment. Accordingly, their numbers will be dictated by the extent to which employment opportunities expand and non-Aboriginal people successfully compete for them. To date, of course, such competition has tended to favour non-Aboriginal personnel and, notwithstanding a range of initiatives that is likely to emerge from the COAG trial to enhance Aboriginal employment outcomes, this structural situation seems unlikely to drastically alter over the projection period, certainly in respect of the more highly skilled occupations. Thus, non-Aboriginal population growth is estimated separately and according to a simple continuation of their current ratio relative to the regional Aboriginal population (0.05). Also, a key demographic feature of this population that is assumed not to change over time is the focus on working age groups.

Table 2.6. Projection of the Aboriginal population of the Thamarrurr Region by five-year age group, 2003–2023

Age (years)	2003	Projection to 2023	Net change	% change
0–4	350	642	292	83.3
5–9	277	567	290	104.7
10–14	303	491	188	61.9
15–19	244	412	168	68.7
20–24	198	342	144	72.9
25–29	143	268	125	87.3
30–34	127	288	161	126.9
35–39	114	224	110	96.8
40–44	78	175	97	124.7
45–49	72	120	48	66.1
50–54	38	100	62	164.3
55–59	26	84	58	223.8
60–64	26	52	26	100.2
65–69	15	41	26	175.5
70–74	8	18	10	123.2
75+	15	9	-6	-41.3
Total	2034	3833	1799	88.5

Source: Author's own calculations

Aboriginal population totals projected to 2023 for the Thamarrurr region are shown in Table 2.6 and Figure 2.6 by five-year age groups, together with numeric and percentage change from the 2003 population. Overall, by 2023, the Aboriginal population is projected to increase by 88 per cent (or 4% p.a.) to reach a population of 3833, an increase of 1800 persons. If we add to this a ratio-based estimate of the future non-Aboriginal population of 212, this produces a total usual resident population projection of 4045 by 2023. Thus, within a generation, Wadeye and its associated outstations will have a population greater in size than present day Nhulunbuy, a mining town in north-east Arnhem Land. As noted above, for core funding purposes, it is more appropriate to employ a service population estimate. This is more difficult to project, but if an assumption is made that the service population will grow at the same rate as the usual resident population then we can estimate an overall service population for the region in 2023 of 4470. Clearly, unlike the many declining country regions in the rural hinterlands of Queensland, New South Wales, Victoria and South Australia, the Thamarrurr region is rapidly expanding in population size. Unless a major upgrading occurs, this trajectory means that Wadeye (along with many predominantly Aboriginal towns across the Top End) will be increasingly anomalous in the Australian settlement hierarchy for being a vibrant and growing medium-sized country town yet with almost none of the basic infrastructure and services normally associated with such places.

Figure 2.6. Projected resident Aboriginal population of Thamarrurr by age and sex, 2023

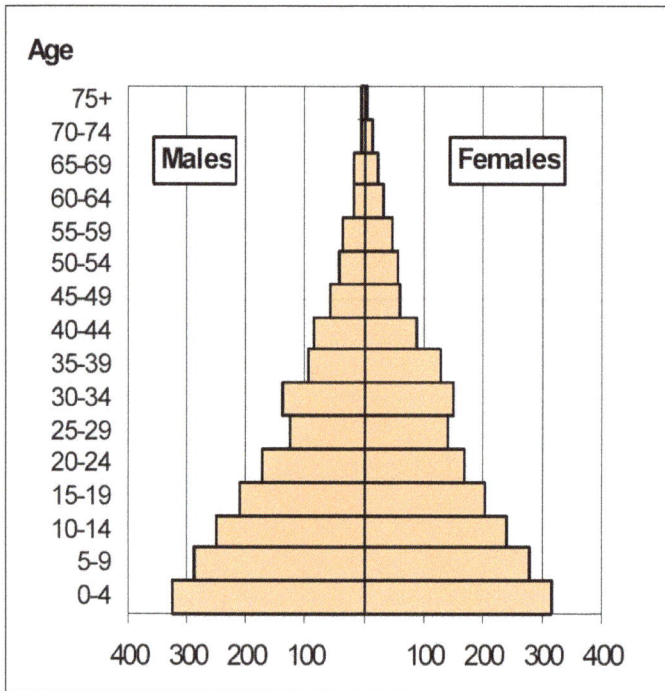

Source: Author's own calculations

From a comparison with Figure 2.4, it can be seen that much of this growth will occur in the working age groups, while Table 2.6 indicates that the population aged between 15 and 49 years will increase by some 1338 over the next 20 years. Also evident is the fact that considerable population momentum remains for further growth beyond the 20-year projection period shown here. While it is true that some ageing of the population pyramid is evident, the chief characteristic in 2023 remains the preponderance of children resulting in a broad base in the age profile. Thus, the only factors that might undermine sustained population growth for probably the next two generations are the prospect of an increase in mortality due to a rise in the incidence of lifestyle diseases (see Chapter 7), a substantial decline in fertility (and, of course, associated major change in social behaviour), or population loss due to permanent migration out of Thamarrurr. At the time of writing, the first of these scenarios seemed possible, while the last two seemed unlikely.

As noted above, social policy and customary age-grading are concerned more with specific age groups rather than the age structure of the whole population, and so Table 2.7 sets out the future age structure of the Thamarrurr regional population according to select social policy target age groups.

Table 2.7. Distribution of resident Aboriginal population by select age groups: Thamarrurr region, 2003 and 2023

Age (years)	2003	2023	Net change	% change[a]
0-4	350	642	292	83.4 (4.2)
5–15	626	1140	514	82.1 (4.1)
16–24	396	672	276	69.7 (3.5)
25–49	530	1075	545	102.8 (5.1)
50+	132	304	172	130.3 (6.5)
Total	2034	3833	1799	88.5 (4.4)

a.   Annual percentage change in parentheses

Source: Author's own calculations

On current projections the greatest numeric increase will be in the population of prime working age between 25 and 49 years, while the highest proportional increase is set to occur among the aged, over 50 years. Both of these broad age groups will more than double in size within a generation from now as the overall age structure of the current Thamarrurr population advances. At the same time, substantial growth will also occur at younger ages, especially among the school age population which corresponds also to the ages at which initiation of young men is a primary concern of Thamarrurr. The slowest rate of growth, however, is expected among those in the transition years between school and work, although much depends here on net migration trends and whether future school leavers will remain in the region or seek opportunities and lifestyles elsewhere.

3. The regional labour market

As with most Aboriginal settlements in north Australia, Port Keats (now Wadeye), was not established with an economic base, nor has it subsequently acquired one, at least not in a manner that is currently sustainable beyond the provisions of the welfare state and associated social services. While the regional labour market has grown in both size and complexity in recent decades as the mission influence has receded and government and market forces have encroached it can be argued that Aboriginal labour force participation has declined. In effect, the past 30 years in this region have witnessed a shift in Aboriginal employment from some historical association with the private sector, as represented by the pastoral industry, to an almost total reliance on the government sector in the form of CDEP. Beyond the latter, there is very limited Aboriginal engagement with mainstream work, with the bulk of the adult population dependent on welfare payments for their income. This is quite distinct from the non-Aboriginal population of Wadeye that is resident in the region solely for the purposes of employment—a structural gap that has significant consequences for relative economic status as well as for consideration of future outcomes in regard to Aboriginal economic participation.

There are three reasons for this. First of all, regardless of whatever targets might be set by the partners to the Thamarrurr agreement in respect of local employment, the major regional impacts on Aboriginal people in terms of raising overall labour force and economic status are likely to depend more on administrative and funding decisions regarding CDEP than anything else. CDEP is by far the main employer and is likely to continue as such given the lack of formal skills among most of the adult population. Future growth of the scheme is dependent on ever-expanding resources from government, while the welfare basis for such funding leaves little scope for advancing employment beyond part-time hours with corresponding low-income return.

Second, CDEP will inevitably form part of any comprehensive planning for regional economic development focused around future activities in Wadeye and surrounding areas. This is because much of the locally based potential workforce for non-CDEP activities would in all likelihood be currently engaged by the scheme and building the necessary skills and experience for alternate work via such employment.

Finally, the extent of reliance on CDEP for generating employment opportunities in the region places a premium on seeking other opportunities for creating and sustaining employment. The essential background to this need is the projected high growth in the Aboriginal working age population and the certainty that CDEP expansion will be insufficient to cater for labour supply.

Regional labour force status

Rates of labour force status drawn from the 2001 Census are shown for Aboriginal and non-Aboriginal residents of the Thamarrurr region in Table 3.1 and these are applied to the 2003 usual resident population count of adults to derive implied labour force status characteristics for 2003 as shown in Table 3.2. Three standard indicators of labour force status are presented, although these are modified here as simple proportions of the population aged 15 years and over:

- *employment/population* ratio, representing the percentage of persons aged 15 years and over who indicated in the census that they were in employment (either in CDEP or mainstream work) during the week prior to enumeration;
- *unemployment rate*, expressed as those who indicated that they were not in employment but had actively looked for work during the four weeks prior to enumeration, as a percentage of those aged 15 years and over;
- *labour force participation rate*, representing persons in the labour force (employed and unemployed) as a percentage of those of working age—shown here in its converse form as a rate of those not in the labour force (NILF).

Table 3.1. Labour force status for residents of the Thamarrurr region: 2001 rates

	Employment/ population ratio		Unemployment rate	Not in the labour force (NILF) rate	Total 15+
	CDEP	Other			
Aboriginal	8.0	5.8	2.0	84.2	100.0
Non-Aboriginal	0.0	95.0	0.0	5.0	100.0

Source: ABS 2001 Census of Population and Housing

Table 3.2. Implied 2003 levels of labour force status for residents of the Thamarrurr region

	Employed CDEP	Employed Other	Unemployed	NILF	Total 15+
Aboriginal	88	64	22	930	1104[a]
Non-Aboriginal	0	63	0	3	66

a.   From Table 2.3

Source: Author's own calculations

There are several difficulties involved in using these census labour force data. First, as they are based on the usual residence count, they exclude any persons missed by the census. Second, they appear to conflict substantially with indications of labour force status from administrative sources. For example, the census indicates that there were 63 individuals employed in CDEP in 2001, whereas ATSIC records show a total of 125 CDEP participants at the time of the census. More striking is the difference between the census count of 16 unemployed persons, compared to the fact that Centrelink recorded 325 Newstart and 129 Youth Allowance customers at the same time, although these were exempt from the work test and so may have been regarded as not in the labour force for census purposes.[3]

Because of these discrepancies, a basic count of regional employment was conducted in Wadeye in November 2003. This revealed a total of 178 Aboriginal people in the Thamarrurr region with jobs—133 funded by CDEP, and 45 funded from other sources. Using these figures, together with Centrelink data on Newstart and Youth Allowance payments for April 2003, a revised set of labour force status levels and associated rates are provided for 2003 in Table 3.3.

Table 3.3. Actual levels and rates of labour force status for Aboriginal residents of the Thamarrurr region, 2003

	Employed		Unemployed	NILF	Total 15+
	CDEP	Other			
Levels					
	133	45	449	477	1104[a]
Rates					
	12.0	4.1	40.7	43.2	100.0

a.   From Table 2.2

Sources: Thamarrurr community census, Thamarrurr employment survey, and Centrelink, Darwin

This suggests an Aboriginal labour force of around 630 which is much greater than that indicated by the census. Of course, much here depends on semantics—are those exempt from the activity test outside of the labour force? Are CDEP participants necessarily in employment according to census definitions? Should a distinction be drawn between CDEP and other jobs given that many CDEP jobs effectively substitute for 'real' jobs in many areas such as education, health, and council services? Indeed, given the administratively determined nature of much Aboriginal economic activity in the region, the boundaries between officially recorded employment, unemployment, and consequent labour force participation, are sufficiently blurred to approach all these data with some caution. They are best seen as rough estimates rather than as robust indicators.

To arrive at a meaningful measure of labour force status, such issues require careful scrutiny on the ground and this provides a useful vehicle for engaging ICCP partners in a dialogue with local working groups concerning the real nature of work, its source funding, and its appropriate measurement. One aspect of this exercise would extend the analysis to consider aspects of economic activity that the census and administrative data sources tend to overlook, namely those customary activities associated with land management, ceremony, and the manufacture of arts and crafts. Just as an example, the 2001

---

[3] According to Department of Employment and Workplace Relations (DEWR) Northern Territory Office, a total of only 39 Wadeye residents have been referred to Intensive Assistance with Job Network since May 1998, but it is not possible to identify those currently serviced by Job Network providers owing to privacy constraints.

Census recorded only 110 Indigenous visual artists in the whole of the Northern Territory, despite evidence from other sources that those participating (admittedly to varying degrees) in the industry through community art centres number in the thousands (Altman 1989; 1999: 83–5; Wright 1999: 25). In Wadeye, the census counted no such occupations, even though the Dirrmu Ngakumarl Gallery in Wadeye and the Wadeye Art and Craft Gallery in Darwin currently support the activities of 10 local artists and have dealt with as many as 126 since 1997. To underscore the local economic importance of activities that are likely to be overlooked by the census, it has been claimed that, by Australian standards, Aboriginal people on some Aboriginal lands are fully employed in the informal sector (Altman & Allen 1992: 142; Altman & Taylor 1989).

Given their labour-intensive nature and widespread occurrence, it is important to consider ways of strengthening these elements of customary economic activity as part of the broad strategy of raising employment levels. A good local example of this is provided by the Thamarrurr Rangers supported by the Northern Land Council's Caring for Country program and by CDEP. This employs 15 local people in land and sea management activities such as mimosa and feral animal eradication, marine species survey, sacred site protection, and in ensuring continuity in local environmental knowledge (Thamarrurr Rangers 2003). Against the background of population projections, the scale of the challenge ahead clearly requires some broadening of the definition and composition of officially sanctioned work to encompass potentially labour-intensive activities associated with land management and cultural heritage, as well as the arts industry. With regard to the latter, it is significant to note that as many as 126 local artists, weavers and carvers have sold products via the Dirrmu Ngakumarl Gallery in Wadeye and the Wadeye Art and Craft Gallery in Darwin since 1997, pointing to substantial potential for economic participation. Presently, however, only 10 individuals are associated regularly with this enterprise—four women and six men—suggesting a need to review options for revitalising the arts industry in the region.

Of particular interest for development planning is the distribution of employment and related labour force status rates by age. As this information was not gathered in the basic 2003 employment survey, these data are drawn from the 2001 Census as well as from CDEP participant records for August 2001. In combining census and CDEP administrative data in this way, the assumption is that CDEP employment figures drawn from administrative data directly affect the numbers shown by the census as not in the labour force. Using these combined data, Figure 3.1 shows the labour force status of broad age groups and reveals that labour force participation (the mirror of those shown here as NILF) peaks in the 35–45 year age group, but even here it is still only 40 per cent. At younger ages, and especially among those in the transition years between school and work, participation in the workforce is very low with barely two per cent of 15–24 year olds engaged in non-CDEP work, and only 15 per cent in CDEP. The vast majority (80%) of these young adults are not in the labour force and are therefore dependent for their income on welfare payments (assuming that these are accessed). The other feature is that participation in non-CDEP work peaks in the older working age group of 45–54 years.

Figure 3.1. Labour force status of each age group: Aboriginal residents of the Thamarrurr region, 2001

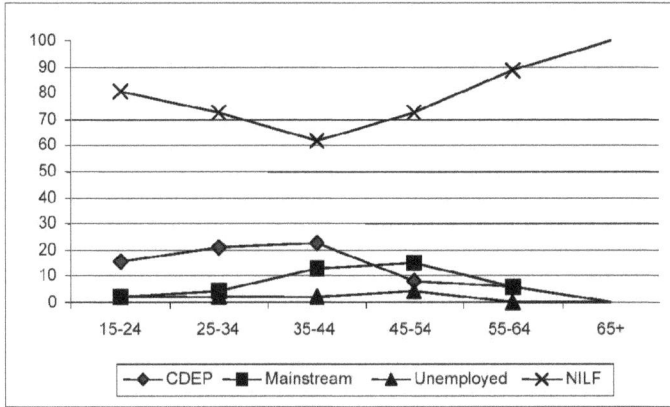

Source: ABS 2001 Census of Population and Housing and ATSIC CDEP branch

If the distribution of different labour force states across age groups is examined as in Figure 3.2, it is apparent that this lack of participation among young adults occurs despite the fact that, overall, CDEP participants tend to be young people with 39 per cent of participants in the 15–24 age group, and with the share of CDEP workers declining with age. The opposite is true, though, in regard to non-CDEP employment with 40 per cent of non-CDEP workers in the 35–44 age range and 25 per cent in the 45–54 age range. Almost half (43 %) of all those who are NILF are in the 15–24 age group.

Figure 3.2. Distribution of labour force status by age group: Aboriginal residents of the Thamarrurr region, 2001

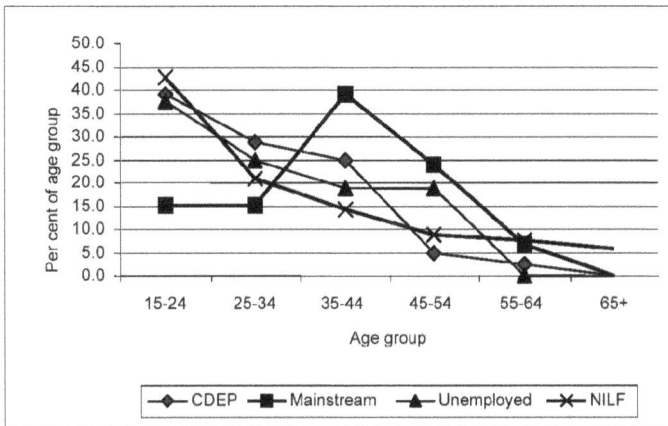

Source: ABS 2001 Census of Population and Housing and ATSIC CDEP branch

Whether there is any transition from CDEP participation at younger ages to mainstream work later on with the former acting as a preparatory skilling phase is not discernable from these data. This is something that could usefully be explored by the Thamarrurr

ICCP working groups. As expected, though, labour force participation is positively correlated with age up to 44 years, but recedes rapidly thereafter indicating a distinctly shortened working-life span. One prospect is that this reflects increased morbidity with advancing age, a proposition that will be tested with hospital separations data.

Dependency ratios

Measures of the potential economic implications of a given age structure can be combined with data on labour force status to produce a range of dependency ratios. These are shown in Table 3.4 for the Aboriginal population of Thamarrurr using the population data for 2003 shown in Table 2.4, and the levels of labour force status for 2003 shown in Table 3.3. Comparison is drawn with the Northern Territory as a whole using 2001 Census data. The *childhood dependency* ratio is the simplest of these measures and expresses the number of children in the population (aged 0–14 years) as a ratio of the working-age population (defined here as aged 15–49 given the prevalence of adult morbidity). Obviously, a ratio of 1.0 would indicate that the size of the two age groups is the same and that there is one person of working age for every child. A figure greater than 1.0 indicates less than one person of working age to each child, and less than 1.0 indicates more than one person of working age to each child. Obviously, this only provides an indication of potential economic providers to dependents as it takes no account of the economically inactive.

Table 3.4. Dependency ratios for the Aboriginal populations of the Thamarrurr region 2003, and the Northern Territory, 2001

	Thamarrurr region 2003	Northern Territory 2001
Childhood dependency[a]	0.95	0.66
Childhood burden	5.2	1.8
Childhood burden (excl. CDEP)	20.7	3.6
Dependency ratio	2.2	3.1
Economic burden	10.4	3.9
Economic burden (excl. CDEP)	44.2	9.1

a. Based on working age population aged 15-49

Source: ABS 2001 Census of Population and Housing customised tables, Thamarrurr community census, and Thamarrurr employment survey

In the Thamarrurr region, the *childhood dependency* ratio is 0.95, which means that the number of children and those of working age is roughly equivalent. This is quite different to the situation in the Northern Territory as a whole where the ratio of 0.66 indicates far fewer children on average to each person of working age. This provides another measure of the relatively youthful character of the regional population.

More refined measures of dependency incorporate some indication of the ability of working age adults to support others. The *childhood burden*, for example, is defined as the ratio of the number of children to the number of employed persons. Once again, a figure of 1.0 indicates parity. According to the data in Table 3.4, there were 5.2 Aboriginal children to each employed adult in Thamarrurr if all those engaged by the CDEP scheme are considered to be in employment. If, however, this calculation is based on those employed only in non-CDEP work, then the ratio is far higher at 20.7. The fact that both of these ratios are much lower for Aboriginal people generally in the Northern Territory underlines the gross lack of employment opportunities in Thamarrurr and the far greater reliance on CDEP as the primary support mechanism for large numbers of child dependents.

Another measure is provided by the *dependency ratio* which represents the ratio of children and economically inactive adults to the labour force (those employed plus those unemployed). Again, using the data in Table 3.4, this produces an average of 2.2 dependents per economically active person, which is fewer on average than in the Northern Territory as a whole reflecting the use of Centrelink data on Newstart payments to construct the Thamarrurr unemployment numbers presented in Table 3.3.

Finally, the *economic burden* is a ratio of the number of children and economically inactive persons (including here those unemployed) to employed persons. This shows that for each employed Aboriginal person at Thamarrurr (including those in the CDEP scheme) there are 10.4 other Aboriginal people who are not employed (including children), a figure more than twice the Northern Territory average of 3.9 persons. If, however, those in CDEP are excluded from the economically active and considered instead as part of the measure of economic burden, then the figure in Thamarrurr rises to a staggering 44 dependents per income earner, compared to a figure of 9.1 for the Indigenous population of the Northern Territory as a whole—almost five times as great.

From a regional planning perspective, then, the youthful Aboriginal age profile is a key demographic feature when set against the relatively poor labour force status of adults. In effect, there are 44 dependents, on average, for each Aboriginal employee in the mainstream labour market. This represents a significantly higher economic burden for the Thamarrurr population than recorded for the Aboriginal population generally in the Northern Territory. Perhaps of more significance, in the local context of access to resources and consumer spending, is the fact that it is massively higher than observed among non-Aboriginal residents of the region with whom Aboriginal residents can draw direct comparison.

Industry and occupation

In the final analysis, employment provides a means to personal income generation, while the amount generated is determined largely by occupational status. In turn, the availability of particular occupations within a region is partly related to the industry mix of economic activities. Thus, the relative distribution of Aboriginal and non-Aboriginal employment by industry and occupational category is a vital feature of participation in the regional labour market. The sole source of employment data classified according to the Australian and New Zealand Standard Industry Classification (ANZSIC) and the Australian Standard Classification of Occupations (ASCO) remains the census. Accordingly,

Figures 3.3 and 3.4 show broad industry and occupational categories of employment for the Thamarrurr region using data from the 2001 Census.

Clearly, the distribution of Aboriginal employment by industry division is quite different from that of non-Aboriginal workers in Thamarrurr. Aboriginal employment is heavily concentrated in government administration, which in effect reflects the census classification of much CDEP employment. Another focus for Aboriginal workers is health and education. By contrast, according to these data, the non-Aboriginal workforce is more widely spread across industry categories, although the overall range is limited and indicates the very simple structure of the local labour market based on providing essential services and administration to a relatively small population. As for occupations, the distribution reflects the skills gap between Aboriginal and non-Aboriginal workers, with most of the former classified as labourers, and far more of the latter as professionals and tradespeople. However, it is interesting to observe that the Aboriginal distribution itself is bimodal with people employed in either professional or intermediate/labouring positions with an absence of employment in trades and advanced clerical jobs.

Figure 3.3. Distribution of Aboriginal and non-Aboriginal employment by industry division: Thamarrurr region, 2001

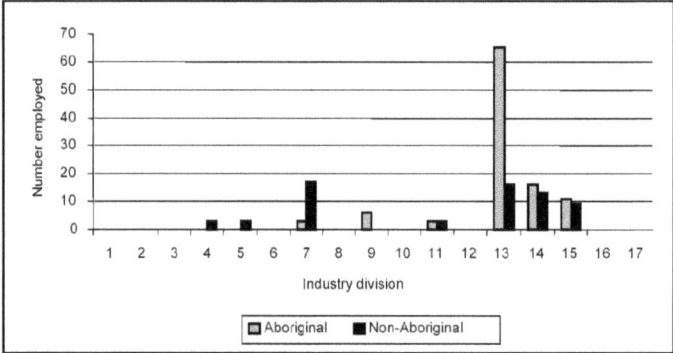

Source: ABS 2001 Census of Population and Housing, customised tables

Key: 1. Agriculture, forestry and fishing; 2. Mining; 3. Manufacturing; 4. Electricity, gas and water; 5. Construction; 6. Wholesale trade; 7. Retail trade; 8. Accommodation, cafes and restaurants; 9. Transport and storage; 10. Communication services; 11. Finance and insurance; 12. Property and business services; 13. Government administration and Defence; 14. Education; 15. Health and community services; 16. Cultural and recreational services; 17. Personal and other services

Figure 3.4. Distribution of Aboriginal and non-Aboriginal employment by occupational group: Thamarrurr Region, 2001

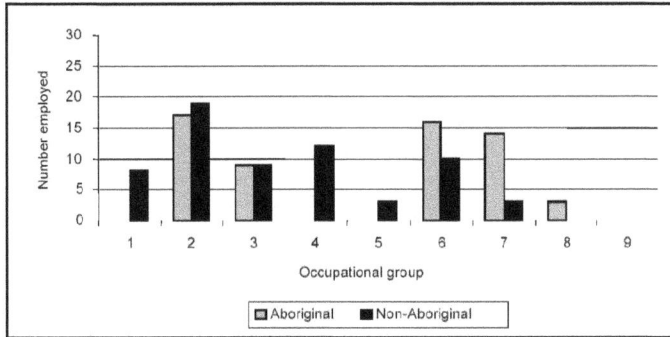

Source: ABS 2001 Census of Population and Housing, customised tables

Key: 1. Managers and administrators; 2. Professionals; 3. Associate professionals; 4. Tradespeople and related workers; 5. Advanced clerical and service workers; 6. Intermediate clerical, sales and service workers; 7. Intermediate production and transport workers; 8. Elementary clerical, sales and service workers; 9. Labourers and related workers.

Leaving aside a likely undercount in the census of numbers employed, there is a tendency for the broad industry and occupation classification to hide a degree of diversity in employment activities at the small area level. Before considering the particular case of CDEP and customary economic activities, it is worth demonstrating this point by examining the range of industries and occupations that are recorded in the census using the detailed industry and occupational classification (based on four-digit coding). Ignoring the actual numbers, as many of these are randomised anyway, Table 3.5 is useful in providing a qualitative depiction of the range of detailed industry activities that collectively describe the composition of the local economy. Key activities emerge such as house construction, the supermarket, takeaway, automotive repair, air transport, credit union, etc. However, even at this fine-grained level, other important industries appear to be unrecorded, such as the sewing centre, arts and crafts, and land management.

Detailed occupations are shown in Table 3.6 and provide another qualitative depiction of the local labour market according to official classification. Despite a wider variety of occupations compared to industries, once again according to these data there are no artists in Thamarrurr, no sewing machinists, no special care workers, no land management workers, and no horticultural workers. This is manifestly not the case, and part of the problem here relates to the census classification of CDEP work.

Table 3.5. Aboriginal and non-Aboriginal employment by detailed industry class: Thamarrurr region, 2001[a]

Industry class	Aboriginal	Non-Aboriginal	Total persons
House construction	0	3	3
Supermarket and grocery stores	0	8	8
Takeaway food retailing	0	5	5
Automotive repair and services, nec	0	3	3
Retail trade, undefined	3	0	3
Air transport, undefined	3	0	3
Credit unions	3	0	3
Business administrative services	0	3	3
Central government administration	3	3	6
State government administration	3	0	3
Local government administration	61	15	76
Education, undefined	0	3	3
School education, undefined	9	0	9
Primary education	3	5	8
Combined primary and secondary education	0	4	4
Health services, undefined	5	3	8
Dental services	3	0	3
Community health centres	4	3	7
Religious organisations	3	0	3
Interest groups, nec	0	3	3
Police services	0	3	3

a. Cell counts of less than three are randomised

Source: 2001 ABS Census of Population and Housing, customised tables

Table 3.6. Aboriginal and non-Aboriginal employment by detailed occupation unit: Thamarrurr Region, 2001[a]

Occupation unit	Aboriginal	Non-Aboriginal	Total persons
General managers	0	3	3
Information technology managers	0	3	3
Professionals, nfd	0	3	3
Registered nurses	0	4	4
Dieticians	3	0	3
Primary school teachers	3	3	6
Special education teachers	3	0	3
Miscellaneous education professionals, nfd	0	3	3
Extra-systemic teachers	6	0	6
English as a Second Language teachers	0	3	3
Welfare and community workers	3	0	3
Urban and regional planners	3	0	3
Occupational and environmental health professionals	3	0	3
Financial dealers and brokers	0	3	3
Shop managers	0	3	3
Customer service managers	0	3	3
Aboriginal and Torres Strait Islander health workers	5	0	5
Police officers	3	3	6
Motor mechanics	0	3	3
Electricians	0	3	3
Carpentry and joinery tradespersons	0	3	3
Plumbers	0	3	3
Greenkeepers	0	3	3
General clerks	5	3	8
Accounting clerks	0	3	3

Occupation unit	Aboriginal	Non-Aboriginal	Total persons
Bank workers	3	0	3
Education aides	5	0	5
Personal care and nursing assistants	3	0	3
Mobile construction plant operators	4	0	4
Intermediate machine operators, nfd	0	3	3
Truck drivers	3	0	3
Storekeepers	3	3	6
Seafarers and fishing hands	3	0	3
Printing hands	3	0	3
Sales assistants	0	3	3
Labourers and related workers, nfd	3	0	3
Cleaners	5	3	8
Nursery and garden labourers	3	0	3
Garbage collectors	8	0	8
Handymen	3	0	3

a.   Cell counts of three or less are randomised

Source: ABS 2001 Census of Population and Housing, customised tables

CDEP activities

One drawback in relation to census-derived industry and occupational data is their tendency to apply blanket classification to CDEP scheme employment. As shown above, this results in a high concentration of Aboriginal employment in government administration, and as labourers. It is also the case that because of the employment substitution effect of CDEP, much work which is classified as CDEP actually covers a wider range of industry and employment categories than is apparent from census coding.

An example here would be CDEP work in a horticulture project. If this were in the mainstream labour market it would be classified under agriculture, fishing and forestry as an industry, and the workers may well be classified as farm hands or skilled agricultural workers depending on the nature of the job. Instead, the tendency is for them to be classified as labourers in local government. The argument here is that census coding of CDEP masks a good deal of potentially significant diversity in the pattern of Aboriginal participation in the regional economy.

One way to demonstrate this is to use information from the activity worksheets of CDEP schemes which provide details of individual economic activities. Among those listed within the region in 2003 are: grading, fencing, road maintenance, plant maintenance and operation, market gardening, media, landscaping, childcare, aged care, environmental health services, sewing, house and other building construction, non-building construction, plumbing and electrical maintenance, pipe laying, painting and decorating, vehicle repair, youth and men's support activities, Centrelink services, clinic assistants, teachers assistants, sport and recreation activities, office assistants, store assistants, and security.

Planning for CDEP in financial year 2003/04 includes 44 workers for local government-type administrative programs, 23 workers for the construction team, 44 workers for community service activities, 13 workers for women's programs, and 40 workers for activities at Palumpa. Given the key role played by CDEP in terms of providing for Aboriginal employment, there is a need to fully acknowledge this diversity of economic activity and explore ways in which vital elements might articulate with economic developments that currently exist, or might materialise, either via direct contracting, sub-contracting and/or joint venturing in some way.

According to data supplied by ATSIC, in August 2003 there were 159 CDEP participants employed by the Thamarrurr CDEP scheme, four of whom were non-Aboriginal. The vast majority of Aboriginal participants were male (103), and 52 were female. Figure 3.5 shows the distribution of these participants by broad age group and reveals that whereas most male workers are relatively young and under 30 years, most female participants are over 30 years.

Figure 3.5. CDEP participants by age and sex: Thamarrurr region, August 2003

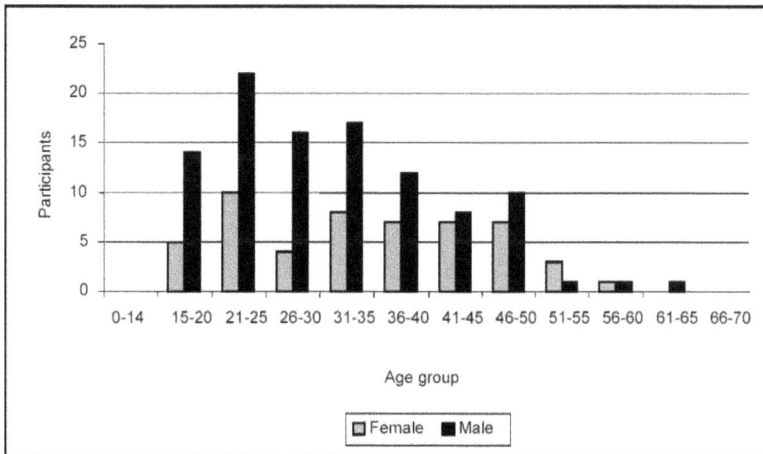

Source: ATSIS CDEP Division, Adelaide

Figure 3.6. CDEP participants as a per cent of male and female age groups: Thamarrurr region, August 2003

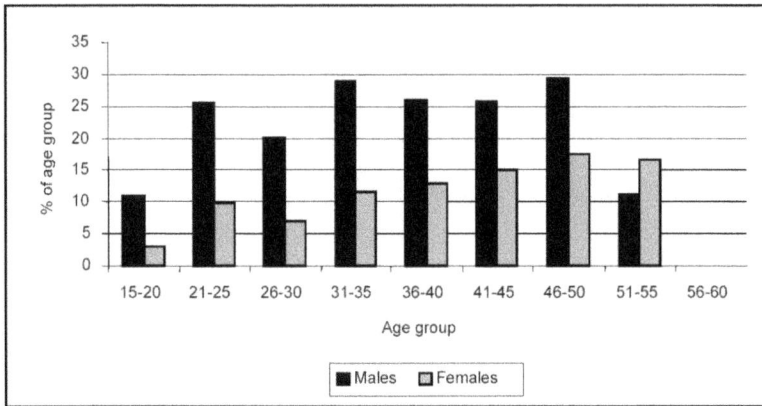

Source: ATSIS CDEP Division, Adelaide

However, raw numbers alone mask the importance of CDEP as a source of employment for older residents. This is shown in Figure 3.6 which indicates the percentage of each age group in the Thamarrurr region employed by CDEP. Among males, the rate of CDEP employment is highest among those aged 46–50 years, and is consistently above 25 per cent for those aged between 31 and 45. At the same time, this is not to deny the significance of CDEP for younger workers with 25 per cent of males in the 21–25 year age group also participating, although the rate among those in the transition years from school to work is relatively low. Among females, there is a direct relationship between age and participation with the importance of CDEP as an employment source generally rising up to age 55.

This essential role of CDEP as a means of generating local employment is further underlined by the lack of alternative opportunities for the unemployed. According to Centrelink data, there were 449 employment services customers in the Thamarrurr region in 2003, 183 of whom had a Job Seeker Classification Instrument (JSCI) score. Despite this, data provided by the DEWR indicate that only 39 Wadeye residents were referred to Intensive Assistance with Job Network providers servicing the Wadeye region since May 1998 (an average of six per year).

Estimating future labour force status

From Table 2.4, the resident Aboriginal population of working age in Thamarrurr is projected to almost double in size from 1104 in 2003 to 2133 by 2023—an increase of 1029, or 93 per cent. Clearly, the economic status of Aboriginal people in the region is largely a function of their continued failure to adequately participate in paid economic activity. What then is the scale of the task ahead if a key aim of the ICCP process is to enhance such participation?

Three future employment scenarios are explored in Table 3.7. The first considers the number of jobs that would be required by 2023 if the 2003 Aboriginal employment to population ratio were to remain unchanged at the current very low rate of 16.1 per cent (inclusive of CDEP). The answer is 343. Thus, the current workforce would need to double in size over the next 20 years simply to avoid any further deterioration in the low employment rate. However, what if the target sought by the Thamarrurr partnership was to double the employment rate, which would bring it in line with the rate recorded for all Aboriginal people in the Northern Territory in 2001? This might be seen as moving to 'normalise' the situation at Wadeye—a term that is now part of the lexicon of planning within the Thamarrurr region signalling the pursuit of equity in social and economic conditions. Against this scenario, the additional jobs required amount to more than 500—a task in order of magnitude that would seem to be way beyond the capacity of current policy settings.

Table 3.7. Extra Aboriginal jobs required in the Thamarrurr region by 2023 against selected target employment rates

Employment/ population ratio in 2003	Base employment 2003	Total jobs required by 2023	Extra jobs required by 2023
16.1[a]	178	343	165
32.2[b]	178	687	509
33.2[c]	178	708	530

a.   The 2003 Aboriginal employment/population ratio inclusive of CDEP

b.   A doubling of the Aboriginal employment/population ratio in 2001

c.   The Northern Territory Aboriginal census-derived employment/population ratio in 2001.

Source: Author's own calculations

4. Income from employment and welfare

Residents of the Thamarrurr region have a number of potential sources of cash income. These range from wage labour in CDEP or in other more mainstream forms of work, unemployment benefit and other benefit payments from Centrelink, agreed payments to traditional land owners, and private income from the sale of art and craft works. Set against these, of course, are routine deductions from income, such as those for house rent and power charges, much of which is now debited at source via Bpay.

Accurate data on income levels, and employment and non-employment sources of income, are notoriously difficult to obtain due to a variety of conceptual problems. For one thing, most available data on income refer to period of time, such as annual or weekly income, whereas the flow of income to individuals and households within the region is often intermittent. Census data, for example, are collected for all sources of income in respect of a 'usual week' and then rounded up to annual income. What might constitute 'usual weekly' income in many Aboriginal households is difficult to determine. On the credit side, there is the likelihood of intermittent employment and windfall gains from sources such as gambling, cash loans, and agreed payments. These sources of income combine with debits, for example due to loss of employment and sometimes welfare payments, to create a highly complex picture even over a short space of time, and one that standard methods of data gathering are likely to misrepresent.

Even if adequate questions were asked regarding income, high levels of population mobility would make it difficult to establish a consistent set of income recipients over a period of time. This is further complicated by job mobility with individuals often employed on a casual or part-time basis and moving into and out of longer-term jobs. As for the circulation of cash between individuals and households, information on this is non-existent. Also lacking are data on expenditure, although a common pattern reported from similar communities is one of cash feast and famine against a background of high costs for essentials such as food and transport (Beck 1985: 89; Taylor & Westbury 2000).

The most comprehensive source of personal income data for the region based on a consistent methodology is available from the census. It should be noted, however, that census data report income in categories, with the highest category left open-ended. Consequently, actual incomes have to be derived. In estimating total and mean incomes, the mid-point for each income category is used on the assumption that individuals are evenly distributed around this mid-point. The open-ended highest category is problematic, but it is arbitrarily assumed that the average income received by individuals in this category was one-and-a-half times the lower limit of the category.

Also, the gross income reported in the census is intended to include family allowances, pensions, unemployment benefits, student allowances, maintenance, superannuation, wages, salary, dividends, rents received, interest received, business or farm income, and worker's compensation received. Whether all such sources are reported in Thamarrurr, or elsewhere for that matter, is unknown. One distinct advantage of census data, however, is that it provides a means by which one estimate of dependence on income from welfare can be derived. This is done by cross-tabulating data on income with labour force status as a basis for distinguishing employment income from non-employment income, the latter being considered a proxy measure of welfare dependence.

Employment and non-employment income

The relative contribution made to total income from employment, as opposed to from other sources, is an important factor in the regional economy. Approximate parity between net incomes derived from social security and those derived from employment (after tax) is likely, unless there is access to well-paying jobs. While it is argued generally for Aboriginal people that the gap between welfare and after-tax earned income is sufficiently low as to discourage job seeking (Hunter & Daly 1998), in the Thamarrurr region clearly the issue is just as much about creating sufficient employment in the first place.

Table 4.1 shows Aboriginal and non-Aboriginal annual average personal incomes as recorded by the 2001 Census. Clearly, employment in the mainstream labour market returns higher personal income compared to CDEP. However, in aggregate, Aboriginal people in mainstream work still lag far behind their non-Aboriginal counterparts with average income levels almost 30 per cent lower due to fewer hours worked and lower occupational status. Even reported Aboriginal non-employment (welfare) income is substantially lower than non-Aboriginal equivalent income. Reasons for this are not clear, but it is worth asking whether this might reflect underpayment of benefits to community residents. Overall, average Aboriginal personal incomes are more than 80 per cent lower than non-Aboriginal income.

Table 4.1. Aboriginal and non-Aboriginal annual average personal income by labour force status: Thamarrurr region, 2001

	Average per category				
	CDEP ($)	Mainstream ($)	Unemployed ($)	NILF ($)	Total earnings per adult ($)
Aboriginal (1)	8926	15 127	8240	8170	8632
Non-Aboriginal (2)	n/a	52 240	n/a	15 600	49 143
Ratio (1/2)	n/a	0.28	n/a	0.52	0.17

Source: Calculated from customised ABS 2001 Census tables

Welfare income

The dollar contribution to regional income from employment and non-employment (welfare) sources estimated from 2001 Census data is shown in Table 4.2. According to these calculations, the total gross annual personal income accruing to adult residents of the Thamarrurr region in 2001 amounted to $10 million. However, only two-thirds of this ($6.6m) went to Aboriginal residents despite the fact that they accounted for 92 per cent of the adult population. Of greater note is the fact that only 16 per cent of the total regional income of $4 million generated by mainstream employment accrued to Aboriginal people. The implications of this are reflected in relative levels of welfare dependency with 82 per cent of total Aboriginal income attributable to non-employment (welfare) sources compared to only three per cent of non-Aboriginal income. If CDEP income is also counted as welfare income owing to its notional link to Newstart Allowance, then the level of Aboriginal welfare dependency rises to 90 per cent.

Table 4.2. Gross annual personal income for Aboriginal and non-Aboriginal adult residents of the Thamarrurr region, 2001

	Aboriginal ($)	Non-Aboriginal ($)	Total ($)	Aboriginal % share of income category
CDEP	535 600	n/a	535 600	100.0
Mainstream	665 600	3 395 600	4 061 200	16.4
Unemployment	107 120	n/a	107 120	100.0
NILF	5 286 320	93 600	5 379 920	98.3
Total	6 594 640	3 489 200	10 083 840	65.4
Welfare share (exc. CDEP)	81.8	2.7		
Welfare share (inc. CDEP)	89.9	2.7		

Source: Calculated from customised ABS 2001 Census tables

While it is not easy to directly compare estimates made from census data with those made from administrative records, in order to gain a clearer picture of the composition of welfare income and to benchmark the census-based estimates of welfare income, inform-ation was obtained from Centrelink on the amounts paid in benefits (excluding CDEP) for a single fortnight as close to the census date as possible (Table 4.3). It should be noted that these data are for the total population owing to difficulties with Aboriginal identi-fication in Centrelink records. It should also be noted that the annualised estimates shown are derived by simply multiplying the fortnightly payments by 26, although there is some justification for this given reasonable stability over time in fortnightly amounts. These data yield an overall estimate of welfare payments of $8.4 million in 2001, which is considerably higher than the census-based estimate of $5.3 million. If we add to this the census-derived figure from Table 4.2 of $4.6 million accruing to non-Indigenous workers, plus CDEP, then the gross personal income for Thamarrurr in 2003 can be es-timated at $13 million.

Table 4.3. Number and amount of Centrelink benefit payments for individuals with a postal address as Wadeye and outstations, 2001

	Number of customers	Total amount of fortnightly benefits paid[a] ($)	Estimated annualised amount paid ($)
Total region	1076	323 238	8 404 188

a.   Based on fortnight ending 20 July 2001

Table 4.4. Fortnightly and annualised Centrelink payments by type and amount for customers with a postal address as Wadeye and outstations, 2003[a]

	Pensions	Newstart	Family	Parenting	Carers	Abstudy	Total
Fortnightly ($)	57 770	125 628	94 843	48 363	1 491	2 235	330 330
Annual ($)	1 502 026	3 266 336	2 465 923	1 257 449	38 763	58 102	8 588 599
No. of customers	143	449	295	146	17	30	1 080

a.   Based on fortnight ending 4 April 2003

Table 4.4 shows the distribution of Centrelink payments by payment type and amount for the fortnight ending 4 April 2003 as at April 2003. While the total number of customers is shown as 1080, and while the payment categories are mostly discrete, there is some overlap between family and parenting payments, and so the actual number of unique customers is probably fewer than shown here. At the same time, with the shift away from payments by cheque, electronic deposits directly into bank accounts now make up 82 per cent of all payments made at Wadeye. As a consequence, and because of frequent short-term population movement in and out of the region, an unknown number of Thamarrurr residents may well be recorded on the Centrelink database with a non-Thamarrurr address and so do not appear in the data shown here. The likelihood, then, is that these data represent a sample, albeit a large one, of the Thamarrurr situation.

While the amounts paid vary from fortnight to fortnight, this variation is only slight and the distribution by payment types shown here has been reasonably stable for the past two years. Thus, the annualised amounts, while estimates only, are fairly robust. Overall, then, an estimated annual total of $8.6 million is paid by Centrelink[4] to residents of Wadeye and outstations in line with their citizen entitlements. The greatest share of this amount ($3.2m or 37%) is allocated as Newstart Allowances for those unemployed. Almost half of all Centrelink customers fall into this category. The next largest group are those in receipt of family payments amounting to $2.5 million (29% of total payments). In line with the youthful age distribution, pensions account for only 17 per cent of all payments, although Abstudy payments represent a miniscule proportion (0.7%) despite the relatively large numbers in eligible age groups. Only 25 individuals over the age of 16 years were in receipt of Abstudy, and only five aged less than 16.

---

[4]This is 55 per cent higher than the census-based estimate of $5.4 million. While both estimates are likely to suffer methodological uncertainty, it does seem that the census substantially under-reported non-employment income.

5. Education and training

There are two broad perspectives against which the purpose and performance of education in the region may be assessed. The first is culturally grounded and considers what Aboriginal people want from education. According to one analyst, with reference to Arnhem Land communities, many Aboriginal people selectively procure aspects of Western education and ignore others that do not suit their needs or aspirations (Schwab 1998). Consequently, what is desired from education in general, and from schools in particular, can be very different to what these western institutions expect. These desires have been conceptualised in terms of the acquisition of core competencies to deal with the non-Aboriginal world, the capacity for cultural maintenance, and access to material and social resources (Schwab 1998: 15).

The second derives from an economic development model and stresses a need to acquire the requisite skills for participation in the mainstream economy. From this perspective, educational outcomes are measured in terms of participation rates, grade progression, competency in numeracy and literacy skills, and (for the Vocational Education and Training [VET] sector), course completion. Given the need to develop a statistical profile of the regional population, the entire focus here is on this second perspective. This is not to deny that skills acquired outside of formal educational processes cannot, and may not, lead to Aboriginal participation in the regional economy in other more informal ways, for example in art and craft production and in land management. The problem for socio-economic profiling is that these more culturally grounded attributes are difficult to quantify and lack readily accessible data sources.

There is no doubt that formal schooling is seen locally as encompassing cultural education, including instruction in Murrin-Patha and, to a limited extent, other local languages. For this reason, although Thamarrurr Regional School (TRS) (formerly Our Lady of the Sacred Heart) remains administered by the Northern Territory Catholic Education Office, it has been a bilingual school since the 1970s with Murrin-Patha forming a lingua franca basis for an introduction to formal education with instruction in English gradually phased in by Year 5 as shown in Figure 5.1 (Reynolds 1994; Walsh 1990). In fact, of course, the Thamarrurr population is multi-lingual, not just bilingual. To varying degrees, aside from Murrin-Patha, five other local languages are used in the Thamarrurr region along with Aboriginal English, Australian English, Kriol, and potentially up to ten other languages from the immediate social network of Thamarrurr people ranging from Kununurra up to Bathurst Island (Walsh 1990). This complex basis for social interaction highlights the importance for TRS of stressing a cultural foundation to pedagogy.

Figure 5.1. TRS bilingual instruction distribution, pre-school to Year 7

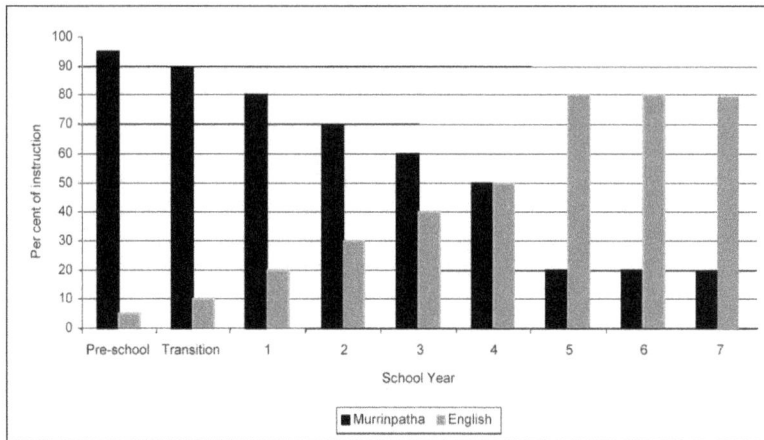

Source: TRS, Wadeye

At pre-school, virtually all instruction and activities are conducted using Murrin-Patha with only 15 minutes per day in English. The ratio of Murrin-Patha to English slowly rises with advancing school years so that by Year 4, instruction is delivered equally in both languages. This changes from Year 5 through to Year 7 with four hours per day presented in English and only one hour in Murrin-Patha, while secondary education beyond Year 7 (mostly by correspondence) is in English only. Culture days are also provided every fortnight to teach local languages other than Murrin-Patha.

The Aboriginal leadership team at TRS views the bilingual program as an essential component of educational provision in the region. Through learning Murrin-Patha cognitively, the aim is to provide a basis for competency in English. This also enables an easier exchange between Aboriginal teachers and pupils, while the infusion of local culture into the Murrin-Patha program by way of storytelling, bush activities, and contextual curricula materials ensures that students are well-grounded in the Murrin-Patha world view. One practical extension of this is a proposal to establish a Junior Rangers program linked to the Caring for Country activities of Thamarrurr Rangers. As for benchmarking learning outcomes, assessment profiles in Murrin-Patha reading, writing, and oral skills are established, although these are more to inform internal school processes regarding staffing requirements and development needs.

Participation in schooling

The TRS is the only school in the Thamarrurr region. Located at Wadeye, it offers formal schooling to Year 7. The school provides for children from pre-school age up to some secondary years, although the latter is provided mostly by correspondence. The nearest secondary school is a newly established independent one at Woolaning near Batchelor, although historically links have long been established with St John's College in Darwin. At the time of writing, three Wadeye residents were enrolled there. Given the current size of the regional school age population (626), and its expected growth over the next 20 years to 1140 (Table 2.5), this lack of full secondary education facilities at Wadeye is anomalous when set against other Northern Territory towns with similar school age numbers.

Most outstations in the Thamarrurr region have no direct access to a school, although there is a small school at Kuy with 20 students and one teacher, while some outstations are trialling an initiative of having a local person teaching children, enhanced by irregular visits from Wadeye-based teaching staff. Some children from outstations in the east of the region attend the Nganmarriyanga (Palumpa) Community School, as well as the school at Daly River. Thus, part of the issue in terms of enrolment and attendance at TRS relates to accessibility for some outstations which are more than two hours travel time by four-wheel drive during the dry season.

Enrolments and attendance

In the first half of 2003, an average of 351 enrolments was recorded at TRS. As in previous years, these enrolments peaked (at 420) in the first month of the school year (February) and progressively declined thereafter to reach 307 by September. Thus, by September only 56 per cent of the region's school age population was enrolled, although at the beginning of the 2003 school year this amounted to 67 per cent. While those attending school are always fewer than the numbers enrolled, the actual rate of attendance remains relatively stable over time at around 51–54 per cent. This is because attendance numbers decline in tandem with enrolment numbers. Clearly the educational impact of relatively low levels of school enrolment is compounded by low school attendance. This is shown in Figure 5.2 which charts the numbers enrolled and numbers attending. Also shown is the attendance rate for each of the school months in 2002 and the first half of 2003. Clearly, aside from the fact that not all children of school age are enrolled, and the fact that even fewer attend classes, there is also a problem of retaining those that turn up at the beginning of each school year.

Figure 5.2. TRS enrolments, attendance, and attendance rates by school month, 2002 and 2003

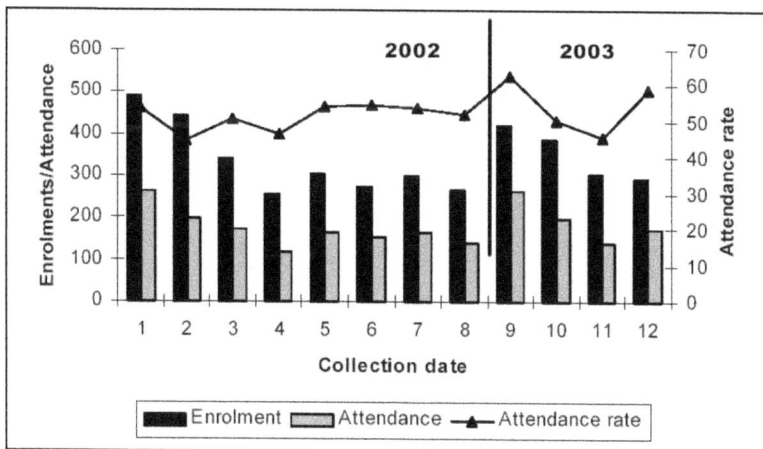

Source: TRS, Wadeye

These shortcomings are further emphasised at the individual grade level with all grades at pre-school and primary levels having fewer than 20 students in attendance by the second half of the school year, and some (Transition and Year 7), having fewer than 10 attendees (Table 5.1). Also apparent is the fact that boys are least likely to be enrolled, and are even less likely to attend classes, with some indication from the September and previous monthly data that this gap widens with age. There are currently 10 girls completing Year 11 via correspondence, and two of these are enrolled in Northern Territory Open Education Centre (NTOEC) courses. Of particular note are those enrolments in foundation studies (Years 7–8) as this is a bridging course for children who have finished primary but are not ready for high school. A further point of note is the current low enrolment in Kardu Kigay, a special school-to-work program designed to retain senior boys (Kigay) at school. This program commenced in 1999 with funding from the Commonwealth Department of Education, Science and Training (DEST), and CDEP and aims to strengthen literacy and numeracy skills as well as self-esteem among young men (aged 16–20 years) with a history of poor school attendance.

Table 5.1. TRS enrolments and attendance by grade level and sex, September 2003

Grade level	Enrolments			Attendance		
	Boys	**Girls**	**Total**	**Boys**	**Girls**	**Total**
Preschool	16	7	23	9	5	14
Transition	11	10	21	3	5	8
Year 1	9	14	23	6	8	14
Year 2	12	16	28	8	11	19
Year 3	9	14	23	6	6	12
Year 4	16	18	34	7	10	17
Year 5	8	15	23	5	10	15
Year 6	13	13	26	8	11	19
Year 7	6	18	24	3	5	8
F/Sa	34	30	64	14	18	32
Senior Girls	n/a	15	15	n/a	10	10
Kardu Kigay	3		3	0		0
Total	137	170	307	69	99	168

a.   Foundation studies

Source: TRS, Wadeye

As for rates of enrolment and attendance by single-year age group, Table 5.2 shows these for September 2003 on the assumption that grade level directly corresponds with single year ages from pre-school at age four to secondary ages from 13–16 years. If this is so, then just over one-third of four-year-olds were enrolled in pre-school and 22 per cent of these actually attended. The peak age for enrolment appears to be among six- and seven-year-olds in Years 1 and 2 as these are the only ages at which enrolments exceed

50 per cent. They also represent the peak attendance rates, with one-third of children at these ages attending.

At the other extreme, barely one-third of secondary age children are enrolled, and only 18 per cent of this age group are actually attending school, although the rate of attendance is lowest among 12-year-olds at only 13 per cent. This reveals that the maximum exposure to education within the population occurs early at ages six and seven, but even at these ages the vast majority of children in the region are not attending school.

Some idea of the depth of non-attendance is provided by statistics collected by TRS on the duration of absences from school among those not attending. This is shown in Figure 5.3 for the 2002 school year. Clearly, there is only a very small group of regular attendees, totalling 57 in 2002, if fewer than 30 days absence in the year is adopted as the cut off. Accordingly, the vast majority (82%) of enrolled students are frequently absent from school for cumulative periods amounting to more than 50 days in the year.

Table 5.2. Estimated population-based enrolment and attendance rates by single year of age: TRS, September 2003

Single year of age	Population (1)	Enrolment (2)	Attendance (3)	Enrolment rate (%) (2/1)	Attendance rate (%) (3/1)
4	62	23	14	37.1	22.6
5	44	21	8	47.7	18.2
6	42	23	14	54.8	33.3
7	55	28	19	50.9	34.5
8	63	23	12	36.5	19.0
9	69	34	17	49.3	24.6
10	58	23	15	39.7	25.9
11	65	26	19	40.0	29.2
12	60	24	8	40.0	13.3
13–16	226	82	42	36.3	18.6

Source: Community Census and TRS, Wadeye

Retention rates

Although data are not available from which to establish grade level retention rates, a key aim of the school is to retain enrolment and attendance through to eventual employment. Success in this area is fairly limited to date with only 11 recent school leavers in mainstream employment and the rest either on CDEP or in receipt of welfare. Of course, to a large degree this reflects the nature of the local labour market with limited formal employment opportunities for relatively unskilled school leavers. However, from a labour market perspective, retention to Year 12 from Year 10 has been shown to have the greatest impact on employment prospects for Aboriginal people (ABS/CAEPR 1996; Hunter 1996), yet the numbers on Year 11 correspondence courses remain very few.

Figure 5.3. Duration of absence from school, TRS 2002

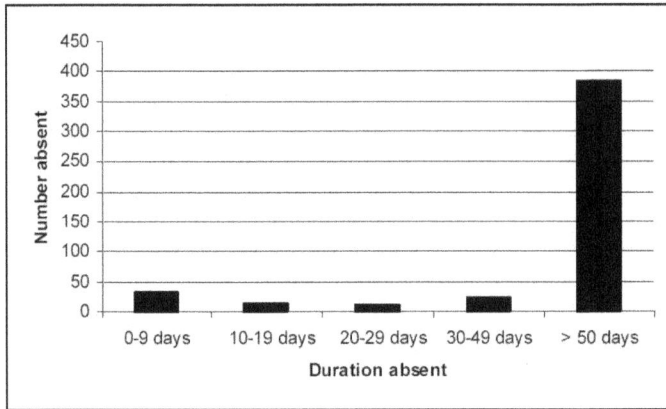

Source: TRS, Wadeye

The impact of low retention is reflected in census data on the highest levels of schooling completed as reported in the 2001 Census and shown in Table 5.3 for adults (those over 15 years). According to these data, only four per cent of adults in Thamarrurr reported Year 11 or 12 completion in 2001. Converting this to a population estimate in 2003 indicates that only 41 Aboriginal adults in Thamarrurr completed school beyond Year 10. By contrast, 56 per cent (an estimated 593) reported less than Year 8 as their highest level and 16 per cent (169) indicated that they had never attended school.

Table 5.3. Highest level of schooling completed among Aboriginal residents of Thamarrurr region, 2003

	Year 8 or below	Year 9	Year 10	Year 11	Year 12	Did not go to school
% of adults[a]	56.1	12.1	11.2	1.2	2.7	16.0
Estimated no.[b]	593	128	118	13	28	169

a.   Based on 2001 Census

b.   Calculated using 2001 Census-based rates against 2003 population

Source: ABS, 2001 Census and Community census

Outcomes

As already noted, from the standpoint of participation in regional economic development, educational achievement is a key prerequisite. While studies reveal a positive relationship between economic status and indicators of educational achievement such as highest level of schooling completed (ABS/CAEPR 1996), an important shortcoming is their lack of measurement of the quality of education outcomes. For example, age at leaving school or highest level of schooling completed does not necessarily equate with school-leaving grade level achievement. In fact, for many Aboriginal students in remote areas of the

Northern Territory, age or grade level is a poor indicator of achievement as many Aboriginal students perform substantially below their age and grade levels in terms of literacy and numeracy competencies (Northern Territory Department of Education [NTDE] 1999). Thus, while data on participation in the education system provide an important indication of access and utilisation, it should be noted that they reveal less about outcomes in terms of demonstrated ability, no matter from what perspective this might be measured.

Table 5.4. Year 3 and Year 5 MAP performance results for reading: TRS, 1999–2001

	1999	2000	2001
Year 3 test			
Number in cohort	19	22	28
Number of participants	19	11	14
Participation rate (per cent)	100.0	50.0	50.0
Number achieving benchmark	0	0	0
Achievement rate (per cent)	0.0	0.0	0.0
Year 5 test			
Number in cohort	11	24	16
Number of participants	11	13	5
Participation rate	100.0	54.2	31.3
Number achieving benchmark	0	0	0
Achievement rate (per cent)	0.0	0.0	0.0

Source: TRS, Wadeye

In the Northern Territory, outcomes from education are measured using benchmarks according to the Multilevel Assessment Program (MAP). This is a curriculum-based assessment that tests students' knowledge and skills in numeracy and reading. It is administered annually under separate arrangements for urban and remote Northern Territory schools. The MAP tests are set at various profile levels—two through to four. At Year 3 level, it is expected that most students will be achieving profile level two, while profile level three is the benchmark standard for students in Year 5. These benchmarks represent an agreed standard of performance that professional educators deem to be the minimum level required for students at particular key stages in their educational development in order to make adequate progress. Prior to the tests, teachers make evaluations of each student before assigning them to a particular test level and exemptions can be, and often are, made if teachers believe that students are likely to achieve near zero scores (NTDE 1999: 156). In accordance with Australian government benchmark reporting requirements, eight-year-old and 10-year-old students were tested equating to Years 3 and 5. The results for reading and numeracy testing at TRS are shown in Tables 5.4 and 5.5 respectively for 1999–2001. Clearly, according to these data, students at TRS have consistently performed very poorly in both reading and numeracy, at both Year 3 and Year 5 levels, both in terms of participation in testing and in achievement.

Table 5.5. Year 3 and Year 5 MAP performance results for numeracy: TRS, 1999–2001

	2000	2001
Year 3 test		
Number in cohort	22	28
Number of participants	11	12
Participation rate (per cent)	50.0	42.9
Number achieving benchmark	0	2
Achievement rate (per cent)	0.0	16.7
Year 5 test		
Number in cohort	24	16
Number of participants	12	3
Participation rate	50.0	18.8
Number achieving benchmark	0	0
Achievement rate (per cent)	0.0	0.0

Source: TRS, Wadeye

Reasons for this are properly the concern of the school, including its Indigenous leadership team, together with parents and the community as now represented by the Thamarrurr working groups on families and youth. However, the school advises that MAP results to date need to be interpreted with caution. This is because up until 2001 TRS students were placed in a grade that fitted their development level. As a consequence, children were often two or three grades behind their urban school peers with whom they were compared in MAP testing, with the result that Wadeye students were seen to be 'failing', as indicated in the data above. At the end of 2001 a decision was made to align students at TRS with their peer groups. This involved children skipping a grade or two (and in some cases more than two). Thus, 2003 is the first year that children have been in the age appropriate class, and for this reason MAP results may not show any indication of improvement for a few years. Children who are in Year 4 now will be better off by the time they reach Year 7 than the Year 7 children in 2003. Thus, 2002 and 2003 have been transition years towards closer alignment between age and grade level, and the outcome should be more meaningful MAP test comparison in the future.

However, even if this leads to a relative improvement in testing outcomes for TRS students, current data suggest a need to consider the implications of literacy and numeracy levels for planning objectives to the extent that these require a future supply of skilled labour for work in mainstream occupations. One implication of poor school performance is evident in the lack of Aboriginal adults in the region with formal qualifications. The only comprehensive data available on this are from the 2001 Census and these can be used to estimate 2003 levels. On this basis, it is estimated that 16 Aboriginal adults have an advanced diploma, 12 have a certificate level qualification, and the vast majority (97%) have no formal qualification. Judging by the school attendance levels, and the literacy and numeracy levels indicated by the recent MAP performance results shown above, there is little indication that this low level of post-school qualification will substantially alter in the near future. At the same time, much depends on participation and outcomes in vocational education and training.

Participation in vocational education and training

Post-secondary education and training leading to the acquisition of formal qualifications is available from the Northern Territory Technical and Further Education (TAFE) system and from private providers. Data on course and module enrolments are available from the Northern Territory Department of Employment, Education and Training (NTDEET) for individuals in their database where Wadeye is indicated as the training provider location. Table 5.6 shows the number and proportion of Aboriginal enrolments recorded at Wadeye in this way for successfully completed courses by course level in 2001.

Overall, 88 individuals successfully completed courses in 2001, most of whom (77 per cent) were female. However, around three-quarters of all successfully completed courses for both males and females were in short miscellaneous enabling courses with no formal certification attached. Only 20 successfully completed enrolments were in certified courses, with all of these (except one Diploma) in Certificate levels I–III. As for the field of study, this was not indicated for the majority of cases (67), while the remainder was in building, and in health and community services. In the same year, a total of 48 enrolments were not successfully completed. Most of these (32) were module-only courses, five were at Certificate I level, seven were Certificate II, and three at Certificate III.

While data on course and module completions were not available beyond 2001, data on course enrolments specified in national training packages were made available for 2002. Overall, in 2002, 44 individuals (19 males and 25 females) were enrolled in nationally accredited qualification courses designed to lead to a qualification specified in a national training package. Most of these (22) were at Certificate I level, six were Certificate II, and 14 at Certificate III. As for the age distribution, all of those in Certificate I courses were aged 15–19.

Table 5.6. Assessable Aboriginal enrolments successfully completed by TAFE course level: Wadeye, 2001[a]

Course level	Males		Females		Total	
	No.	%	No.	%	No.	%
Module only	14	70.0	53	78.0	67	76.1
Certificate 1	3	15.0	3	4.4	6	6.8
Certificate 2	1	5.0	7	10.3	8	9.1
Certificate 3	1	5.0	5	7.3	6	6.8
Certificate 4	0	0.0	0	0.0	0	0.0
Diploma	1	5.0	0	0.0	1	1.1
Total	20	100.0	68	100.0	88	100.0

a. Excludes Aboriginal status not stated

Source: NT DEET, Darwin

Enrolments in other nationally accredited courses, not leading to a qualification specified in a national training package were more numerous (157). Most of these trainees were female (96), and they were either at Certificate I level (82), or involved a basic statement of attainment not recognised by level (73).

As for outcomes, key performance measures in the VET sector tend to relate to efficiency, effectiveness and quality. In relation to the effectiveness of the training system, the key indicator is the rate of successful completion of modules—the components from which courses are constructed. In 2001, a total of 207 module enrolments were recorded. Of these, 124 (60%) were successfully completed (75 by females, and 49 by males), and 83 (40%) were not successfully completed (56 by females and 27 by males). In the successfully completed modules, the field of study was mostly not stated (62%), while most of the remainder was in building, health and community services, and TAFE multi-field education courses.

6. Housing and infrastructure

One of the priority issues identified by the people of Thamarrurr under the regional ICCP agreement is housing and construction. Under the agreement, the goal of raising housing standards in the region to acceptable levels is vested in the housing and construction working group which has a firm basis for its activities in the form of the *Thamarrurr Region Business Plan for Community Housing 2002–2006* (TRBP). As a long term operational plan, this has as its goal the achievement of average occupancy rates of seven persons per dwelling, although in the context of environmental health standards and the need for basic functional requirements in meeting housing standards, the actual targets are, of necessity, more complex than this simple formulation. Adjunct to this plan is a spatial planning objective of intra-regional decentralisation enabling family groups to reside more permanently on country.

Housing

Difficulty in establishing a precise measure of housing need arises from the stock and flow nature of housing assets. This is captured in the data shown in Table 6.1 which indicates that the Thamarrurr Regional Housing Authority manages 217 dwellings in the Thamarrurr region (this includes eight houses at the new Manthatpe subdivision and 18 improvised dwellings) to provide for an Aboriginal service population of some 2260. In addition, there are 39 government-owned dwellings occupied by teachers, police, health staff and other government workers.

In terms of a simple occupancy rate calculated as the number of dwellings to service population, the Aboriginal housing stock accommodates 11.0 persons per dwelling. However, as also shown in Table 6.1, 17 of these dwellings require major repair, and 54 need to be demolished (33% of the stock) leaving only 148 habitable homes. If the substandard dwellings are excluded from the stock, the occupancy rate rises to 16 persons. At the same time, a few of the structures referred to here as dwellings (especially at outstations), are more appropriately described as shelters and not houses, although precise determination of what constitutes a 'house' for the purposes of calculating occupancy is open to interpretation. This is an issue that will no doubt be addressed by the Thamarrurr Housing and Construction priority working group. Suffice to say, that by most standards, the actual stock of satisfactory housing might well be reduced further below 136, although the current working figure used by the Thamarrurr Regional Housing Authority is 157.

Also problematic is the impact of population mobility. Table 6.1 shows Aboriginal service population estimates for Wadeye and separate outstations. The term, estimates, is used here to reflect the inherent uncertainty of establishing a population figure for a given locality owing to the frequency of mobility between localities, especially between Wadeye and outstations. The figures shown indicate the numbers that were allocated to places from the community survey and in administrative records as at August 2003. However, it should be noted that the Wadeye figure is substantially inflated in the wet season owing to a shift of population from outstations to town. Likewise, the population at some outstations can rise substantially for short periods (even daily) owing to movements of people out of town as well as from outside of the region. Within Wadeye itself, and particularly within the six main camp areas, substantial inter-household mobility occurs with numbers resident at any given dwelling rising and falling according to circumstance. The data shown in Table 6.1 therefore represent an essentially static view of a highly dynamic situation. From a planning perspective, the best that can be said is that these data point to a minimum service population for the town of Wadeye of around 2050, and a peak service population for outstations of around 200. At times, though, the numbers resident in Wadeye may approximate the regional total of over 2200 due to periodic movements into town. In terms of housing provision, these temporary relocations of people add substantially to pressures on accommodation, not least via increased wear and tear on housing stock and habitability (functionality), mostly by virtue of intense periods of overuse.

Table 6.1. Thamarrurr Regional Council housing stock and Aboriginal service population by location, 2003

Location	Population	Dwellings	In need of: Minor repairs	Major repairs	Replacement[b]
Wadeye	2045	154[a]	106	15	33
Ditchi	5	2	0	0	2
Nadirri	25	6	1	0	5
Perrederr	20	8	8	0	0
Ngardinitchi	6	3	0	0	3
Wudapuli	30	6	4	0	2
Nemarluk	47	6	5	0	1
Merrepen	19	6	6	0	0
Kultchill	0	0	0	0	0
Kuduntiga	3	3	0	0	3
Kuy	15	5	4	0	1
Ngarinthi	0	1	1	0	0
Nama	11	1	1	0	0
Ngunithak	6	2	2	0	0
Tchindi	0	0	0	0	0
Nangu	0	1	1	0	0
Wumuirdin	0	1	1	0	0
Yederr	0	3	0	1	2
Fossil Head	12	4	4	0	0
Kubiyirr	5	2	0	0	2
Old Mission	9	4	3	1	0
Nama	2	1	1	0	0
Total region	2260	219	148	17	54

a. Includes eight new houses at the Manthatpe subdivision

b. Includes 18 improvised dwellings

Source: Thamarrurr Regional Housing Authority, and Thamarrurr community census

This intra-community mobility, combined with movements into Wadeye from outstations and from elsewhere such as Palumpa, makes it very difficult to assign many individuals to particular dwellings. Having said that, while the average number of persons per functional dwelling in the region amounted to 17, there are several dwellings that cater for more than this number. While the process of assigning individuals to particular dwellings remains a task of the housing and construction working group, at least 48 dwellings had more than the average number of occupants in 2003, with one having as many as 22. However, as noted above, this situation varies over time. According to the Thamarrurr Regional Housing Authority, a 2002 housing occupancy survey of Wadeye recorded six dwellings with more than 20 occupants and one with 26. Because of this fluidity, average occupancy provides the most useful underlying baseline measure.

The major response to such inadequacies was led by the Commonwealth and developed out of the National Aboriginal Health Strategy (NAHS) in 1990. This recognised an essential link between health outcomes and the provision of housing and infrastructure to acceptable minimum standards. Accordingly, funding allocations in the initial years of the NAHS primary health and environmental health programs included amounts directed at housing and infrastructure services within ATSIC's Community Housing and Infrastructure Program (CHIP). However, a review of CHIP in 1994 identified a range of problems, including a failure to address housing and infrastructure needs in a holistic way. Because of the short-term nature of the program-based approach to funding, communities were being required to structure housing needs to the CHIP program rather than the other way around (ATSIC 1994). A key response to these criticisms was the establishment in 1994 of the Health Infrastructure Priority Projects (HIPP) program to pilot new delivery arrangements for the construction of Aboriginal community housing and infrastructure.

A significant outcome from NAHS/HIPP and Indigenous Housing Authority of the Northern Territory (IHANT) spending in Thamarrurr has been the establishment of the Manthatpe subdivision with the construction of eight new houses in 2003 and planning space for a further 16. This housing is earmarked for members of the Yek Maninh and Wentak-Nganayi clans and as such represents a prototype development in the context of Thamarrurr regional planning as the first attempt to locate families on country away from Wadeye town.

While the high occupancy rate reflects larger Aboriginal household size and, in part, a cultural preference for extended family living arrangements, it is fundamentally a measure of the inadequacy of housing stock available to accommodate the regional population. To acquire a better sense of the adequacy of housing, occupancy rates must be set against dwelling size and one measure of this is provided by the ratio of available bedrooms to the population in dwellings (Table 6.2). Overall, in the region, the CHINS recorded a total of 484 bedrooms in 2001. Since that time, construction of new housing at the Manthatpe subdivision has added further bedrooms. However, many rooms within the housing stock remain in substandard dwellings and include improvised bedrooms. By excluding these, the current (2003) working figure for the number of available bedrooms in Thamarrurr is 451, which translates into an average of five persons per bedroom.

Future housing needs

Usually, in estimating housing needs, a model of future household formation by size of household would be required on the assumption that individual households occupy individual dwellings. This is not possible in the Thamarrurr region given the highly fluid nature of household composition and its typical distribution across more than one dwelling. Thus, to estimate future housing needs, a simple equation of projected persons per dwelling is employed using the population projections data shown in Table 2.6.

To begin with, there is already a substantial need for additional housing. In the current TRBP it is estimated that an extra 206 dwellings would be required to 'normalise' the situation at seven persons per three-bedroom dwelling. However, with rapid population growth this estimate is not static and will grow in line with resident numbers.

Table 6.2. Dwellings by bedroom size: Wadeye and outstations, 2003

	Population	No. of bedrooms				Total bedrooms	Persons per bedroom
		2	3	4	5		
Wadeye	2101	33	71	22	2	377	5.6
Ditchi	8	2	0	0	0	4	2
Nadirri	6	4	0	0	0	8	0.75
Perrederr	20	7	1	0	0	18	1.1
Ngardinitchi	0	3	0	0	0	6	0
Wudapuli	30	2	2	0	0	10	3
Nemarluk	35	3	2	0	0	12	2.9
Merrepen	25	2	3	0	0	13	1.9
Kuy	15	4	0	0	0	8	1.8
Yederr	0	3	0	0	0	6	0
Fossil Head	12	3	0	0	0	6	2
Kubuyirr	0	2	0	0	0	4	0
Old Mission	6	3	1	0	0	9	0.7
Nama	2	0	1	0	0	3	0.7
Total region	2260	71	81	22	2	484	4.7

Source: Thamarrurr Regional Housing Authority, and Thamarrurr community census

Because the service population is used in estimating housing needs, one difficulty in calculating future needs lies in establishing likely service population numbers as the projections provided in Table 2.6 refer to usual resident numbers only. There are no clear methods available here, and so the service population is simply assumed to grow in tandem with the usual resident population. On this basis, the Aboriginal service population is estimated to reach 4260 by 2023. Using this figure, and the current occupancy rate of 16 persons per functional dwelling, it can be estimated that an extra 122 dwellings would be required by 2023 simply to maintain the current occupancy at this very high level. In this case, the stock of functional dwellings would need to total 266 (as opposed to 144) within the next 20 years.

However, as set out in the TRBP, the intention is to normalise the situation and achieve a ratio of at least seven persons per dwelling. If this were to be achieved, a total of 465 extra dwellings would be required by 2023, producing a total stock of 609 functional dwellings. The reference here to 'functional' dwellings is important, as this indicates that housing needs include more than just the provision of shelter. They also include aspects of functional utility for healthy living.

Another approach to housing needs assessment has been developed by IHANT which applies a bedroom need index based on the housing needs model developed initially by Jones (1994). In recognition of the multidimensional nature of Indigenous housing need, IHANT also incorporates other dimensions of need and so the formula for assessment becomes an amalgam of the following:

Overcrowding and homelessness:

- number of additional bedrooms needed for the population against a standard of 1.8 per bedroom
- count of the number of temporary or improvised bedrooms to be replaced

Stock condition:

- count of the bedrooms needing to be replaced due to poor condition
- count of the number of bedrooms needing major repair or renovation

On this basis, the number of new bedrooms required in the Thamarrurr region to meet IHANT guidelines in 2003 amounted to 846 with 21 bedrooms requiring replacement leading to an overall estimate of total additional bedroom need of 867. At an average cost of $60 000 per bedroom, this produces a total cost for the normalisation of housing stock of $52 million.

Environmental health infrastructure

As with the measurement of housing need, the status of environmental health infrastructure requires a detailed assessment of functionality and adequacy set against agreed normative criteria. At the time of writing, two data sources were available for the Thamarrurr region to establish this—the CHINS, and IHANT's Environmental Health Survey. Of these sources, the data from the 2001 CHINS are the least useful for compiling a detailed inventory of the condition of environmental health infrastructure as they report only at a community-wide level and in general terms. Thus, while information on key items such as water supply, sewerage, drainage and solid waste disposal are provided, this is more in the form of simply noting the existence or otherwise of infrastructure rather than assessing its functionality and adequacy in any detail. Likewise, CHINS data do not allow for the proper assessment of activities related to such issues as dust control, animal health and quality of waterways. For example, with regard to dust control, all that is available from the CHINS is the fact that a certain number of permanent dwellings are on sealed roads. Thus, while this provides some indication of the likely extent of dust mitigation as an issue, it is far from adequate as a baseline indicator.

The IHANT survey data provide for a more accurate picture of housing functionality as they are based on physical inspections of each individual dwelling and framed around the notion that Aboriginal community housing and infrastructure should be designed, constructed and maintained to support healthy living practices, principles now firmly embedded in policy following the pioneering work of Pholeros, Rainow and Torzillo (1993) in the Pitjantjatjara Lands. A total of nine such practices are identified, in descending order of priority in terms of impact on health outcomes: capacity to wash people, wash clothes and bedding, remove waste safely, improve nutrition, reduce crowding, separate people from animals, reduce dust, control temperature, and reduce trauma. Each of these refers to different aspects of the functionality of dwellings and their related infrastructure. For example, if the focus is on improving nutritional standards and practices, then 'healthy home hardware' refers to the provision of adequate facilities to store, prepare, and cook food. It also extends to water quality and quantity as a lack of these may lead individuals to purchase bottled water or other beverages, thereby adding to expenditure and increasing reliance on soft drinks and cordials.

Accordingly, the National Indigenous Housing Guide (Commonwealth of Australia 1999) and the IHANT guide to environmental health standards for remote communities in the Northern Territory (Northern Territory Government 2001) include a range of detailed design and functionality standards related to these healthy living practices. The key functional area with most guidelines is that involving the supply, usage and removal of water: six of the nine healthy living practices are dependent on these. However, even seemingly obscure health-related housing functions include a wide range of design, maintenance and infrastructural features that require attention (Commonwealth of Australia 1999: 49–57). For example, guidelines for improved nutrition include consideration of the following factors that provide an indication of the detailed assessments involved in measuring functionality:

- *Different ways of cooking:* Given often-crowded dwellings and failure of cooking equipment, it is common for many different age groups to share the cooking facilities of a house. At the same time, each group may have a different preference for cooking. For example, younger people may use a microwave oven; middle-aged people may use a stove or drum oven and barbecue, older people may prefer the ground and a fire for cooking. To this extent, there is a need to consider how many 'kitchens' each house may need.

- *Electric cooking: stoves and hotplates:* Electric hotplate cooking is one of the major sources of energy use in a house. To control costs, stove timer switches can be installed to cut off power after a set period. It has also been found that solid hotplates are more robust than coil elements.
- *Operational fridges:* Poorly performing fridges can lead to food spoiling and food poisoning as well as to high-energy costs. A number of simple directives can be applied to assist in overcoming these problems, for example ensuring that the fridge is located in a thermally efficient area and that door seals are regularly maintained. However, one problem with fridges in overcrowded households is frequent use, and the only solution here is to provide either more fridges or lower density housing.
- *Kitchen cleaning and maintenance:* The design and detailed specification of the kitchen area, joinery, and appliances can make cleaning easier by reducing cleaning effort and access for insects and vermin.
- *Food storage:* Low shelves and cupboards are easily accessed by dogs and children, or are unused or used to store non-food items. Consideration should be given to providing high shelves and cupboards and lock-up pantries that are insect-proof and well ventilated.

Figure 6.1. Distribution of environmental health hardware items requiring major repair or replacement: Thamarrurr, 2002

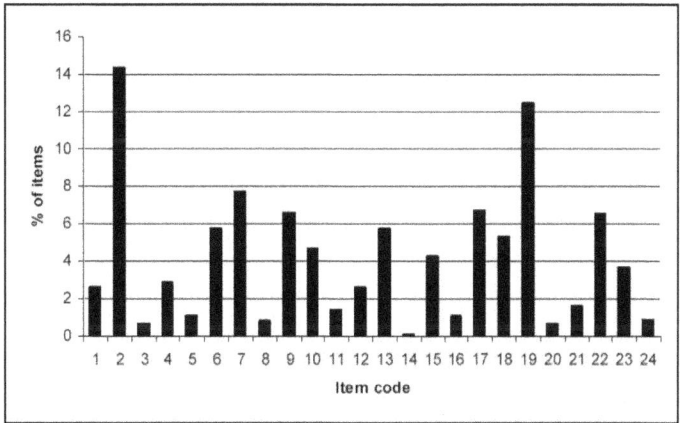

Key: 1. Basin; 2. Bench/shelf; 3. Cistern; 4. Door; 5. Drainage; 6. Electrical; 7. Boundary fence; 8. Floor drainage; 9. Food storage; 10. General structure; 11. Hot water service; 12. Kitchen floor; 13. Oven; 14. Septic tanks; 15. Shower; 16. Sink; 17. Storage; 18. Stove top; 19. Taps; 20. Toilet pan; 21. Trough; 22. Utensil storage; 23. Washing machine; 24. Water supply

Source: Northern Territory Government, Indigenous Housing Environmental Health Survey, customised tables

Clearly, then, data needs are very detailed, not just for the purpose of establishing the range and level of health hardware needs for each dwelling in the first instance, but for the ongoing monitoring of needs as they develop so as to inform maintenance programs.

The most recent IHANT environmental health survey in the Thamarrurr region was conducted in 2002/03. This reports on the adequacy of up to 96 individual items of health hardware for each room of each dwelling, as well as on the exterior condition of individual houses and associated yards and services. In line with the National Aboriginal Housing Guide these items are listed according to their contribution to healthy living practices such as ability to cook and prepare food, ability to wash clothes, and ability to wash people. In Thamarrurr, just over 8000 individual hardware items were reported on. In more than a quarter of cases (27%), this was to indicate that the item simply did not exist (for example a bedroom with no door, or a laundry with no washing machine). In five per cent of cases it was to report the need for minor repairs, and in 12 per cent of cases the item was found to be a health or safety hazard and was in need of either major repair or replacement. Thus, almost half of all the health hardware in Thamarrurr was found to be deficient in some way. Figure 6.1 provides an indication of the type of health hardware items reported as in need of major repair or replacement. This reveals that the most common deficiencies are related to storage (items 2, 9, 17, and 22) and taps (item 19), although it is striking that the distribution is across much of the range.

7. Health status

Information on the health status of Aboriginal people is gathered as a matter of course in the day-to-day operation of the health care system in the Northern Territory. Information at the regional level, as in the case of Thamarrurr, is not routinely available in the public domain. Consequently, data on the current health status of the Thamarrurr population was compiled, summarised, and made available by the Northern Territory Department of Health and Community Services (NTDHCS) in their role as a partner to the ICCP trial, and in response to a special request on behalf of the Thamarrurr Council.

As is often the case, there is a need for aggregation of some health data to at least SLA level (roughly equivalent to the Top End West Primary Health Care Access Program [PHCAP] zone) in order to produce statistically reliable health indicators. This is because of the relatively small size of the Thamarrurr population in a statistical sense. While this inevitably involves some loss of geographic detail, it nonetheless enables the estimation of some key indicators (notably here, the mortality rate), that otherwise would be unavailable. Morbidity rates, based on hospitalisation data, are calculated for Thamarrurr itself, although with a fairly brave proviso (following the evidence in Chapter 2) that estimated resident population figures and hospital admissions data are assumed to be sufficiently compatible for the former to be employed as a meaningful denominator for the latter.

Estimation of mortality

The mortality rate can be used as a proxy measure of health status. While the usual residence of Aboriginal people is recorded in death statistics held by the ABS these are coded only to the SLA level. In the case of Thamarrurr, this refers to the Daly SLA. Between 1997 and 2001, a total of 88 Indigenous deaths were officially recorded for this area—59 male, and 29 female. With these data, it is possible to calculate a standardised Aboriginal mortality ratio for the Daly SLA to account for the quite different age structure of the Aboriginal population compared to the standard. The assumption here is that the resulting rate would be very similar to that calculated for Thamarrurr, if such a calculation were possible.

Given the relatively small size of the Aboriginal population in the Daly SLA, and the consequent unreliability of age-specific death rates, it is appropriate to apply indirect standardisation as is the practise of the ABS (ABS 2002a: 107). This is calculated by applying published age- and sex-specific death rates for the total Australian population (ABS 2002a: 50) to the 2001 Daly SLA Indigenous ERP age/sex distribution. An annual figure for deaths in the Daly SLA is then estimated by averaging recorded deaths over the period 1997–2001 to account for annual variation. This observed figure of 18 Aboriginal deaths for the region is then compared to the expected number (five) derived from the application of the standard age-specific death rates. This produces a standardised mortality ratio for the Aboriginal population of 3.6, indicating in excess of three times more Aboriginal deaths in the region than would be expected if the mortality profile observed for the total Australian population were to apply.

In terms of an indirectly standardised Aboriginal death rate for the Daly SLA, this translates into 24 deaths per 1000, which is 18 per cent higher than the equivalent indirect rate of 20 deaths per 1000 calculated for Aboriginal people in the Northern Territory as a whole (Table 7.1). Higher male mortality accounts for all of this difference. Compared to the total non-Aboriginal population of the Northern Territory, overall Aboriginal death rates in the Daly SLA are four times higher. The comparable figure for all Aboriginal people in the Territory is 3.4 times higher. It is not surprising, then, to discover that the median age at death for Aboriginal people in the Daly SLA was only 46 years.

Table 7.1. Aboriginal and non-Aboriginal indirect standardised death rates[a] for the Daly SLA and Northern Territory, 2001

	Male	Female	Total pop.
Aboriginal Daly SLA	38.2	12.2	23.8
Aboriginal Northern Territory	27.2	14.5	20.2
Non-Aboriginal Northern Territory	N/a	N/a	6.0

a.   Per 1000

Source: Calculated from ABS Deaths registration data, and information in ABS (2002a: 35, 87)

Cause of death

Cause of death data are coded using the World Health Organisation (WHO) method of disease classification that follows the Ninth Revision, International Classification of Diseases (ICD9) up to July 1999, and the ICD10 classification thereafter. Briefly, the ICD consists of 17 primary disease chapters plus two supplementary classifications dealing with external causes of injury and poisoning, and contact with health services. The ICD10 comprises 21 chapters, incorporating the two previous supplementaries.

Ideally, cause of death for the Aboriginal population of Thamarrurr region would be identified using these classifications. However, the ABS does not provide deaths data below SLA level and direct information on the Thamarrurr population is therefore not available. One option, then, would be to use data for the larger Daly SLA on the assumption that this would be representative of the situation at Thamarrurr. However, only 88 Indigenous deaths were officially recorded for this larger area in the five years between 1997 and 2001 resulting in too few deaths to provide a meaningful distribution across categories.

Evidence from the Northern Territory as whole points to the fact that excess deaths among Aboriginal people are mostly attributed to diseases of the circulatory system, respiratory diseases, endocrine disorders (especially diabetes), neoplasms, and external causes. These five disease categories alone accounted for 75 per cent of Aboriginal deaths in the Northern Territory between 1999 and 2001 (ABS/Australian Institute of Health and Welfare [AIHW] 2003: 193–8), and there is no reason to doubt that a similar profile exists for Thamarrurr. Such a profile of mortality typifies the trend towards 'lifestyle' diseases as the primary cause of Aboriginal death, and this underlines the importance of collaborative links between the new Thamarrurr regional governance structures and the Wadeye clinic, especially with the recent appointment to the latter of a chronic disease coordinator (with a focus on diabetes management), a drug and alcohol nurse, and a child health nurse (NTDHCS 2003). One option here for baseline profiling, would be to apply an aetiological fraction methodology to estimate the proportion of illness or injury that can be attributed to a particular risk factor. The two risk factors commonly measured in this way are poor nutrition or alcohol consumption (Holman et al. 1990; Lester 1994: 223; Unwin et al. 1997). However, this requires that alcohol and diet-related diseases (including injuries in the former case) are separately identified using appropriate ICD codes. Unfortunately, the level of detail required precludes this possibility for the Thamarrurr population.

Hospital separations

Hospital separations data for patients from Thamarrurr (defined as those who indicated in the hospital admissions process that a locality within Thamarrurr was their usual place of residence) were provided by NTDHCS for unique patients cumulated over the period 1998–2002, and for admitted patient separations reported in each financial year and aggregated over 1998/99–2001/02. These numbers were provided according to Major Diagnostic Category (MDC) as used in the Australian Refined Diagnosis Related Group (AR-DRG) classification. These data form the basis for compiling a profile of major morbidity for the regional population. However, because the focus is on conditions serious enough to warrant hospitalisation, they do not provide a full measure of the burden of ill health in the region. An indication of this is provided by data from the Chronic Disease Register as recorded by District Medical Officers on visits to Wadeye.

Before considering the hospitalisation data in detail, it is important to note that the number of admissions far exceeds the number of individuals admitted. This is obviously because many people are admitted more than once. Among Aboriginal residents of the Thamarrurr region, a total of 2929 hospital separations were recorded between 1998 and 2002. However, these separations were generated cumulatively by just 1460 individuals producing an average of 2.01 separations per patient. Table 7.2 shows the numbers of patients and separations by broad age groups (at least for those whose age was available). By far the largest number of both patients and separations occur among infants and young children. Of course, this is to be expected given the age distribution of the population, and so it is more meaningful to employ rates of morbidity, particularly in the context of baseline profiling.

Table 7.2. Number of Aboriginal hospital patients and separations: Thamarrurr region residents, 1998–2002

Age group	Patients			Separations		
	Male	Female	Total	Male	Female	Total
0-4	296	256	552	380	335	715
5-14	85	70	155	110	81	191
15-24	41	211	252	42	374	416
25-34	53	163	216	61	313	374
35-44	26	94	120	34	314	348
45-54	17	48	65	18	377	395
55+	29	71	100	35	485	500
Total	547	913	1460	680	2279	2939

Source: NTDHCS, Darwin

Calculation of such rates is not straightforward owing to data quality issues. However, using the four-year cumulated data provided for unique patients by broad age group, it is possible to approximate age-specific hospitalisation rates by taking an average of the four-year numbers and using the ABS ERP as the denominator as stipulated by the NTDHCS for the calculation of rates. The result is shown in Figure 7.1. Given the uncertainties inherent in this approach, the rates shown here are indicative only, although they reveal an expected pattern of age-specific morbidity.

Figure 7.1. Apparent age-specific hospital patient rates: Aboriginal population of Thamarrurr region, 1998–2002[a]

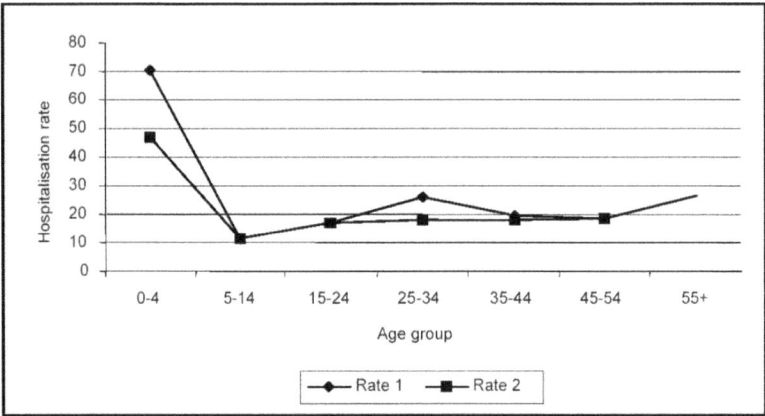

a.   Based on unique patient numbers

Two rates are shown. Rate 1 includes all unique patients and thus incorporates those hospitalised as newborns and neonates (MDC 15), as well as women for childbirth (MDC 14). Not surprisingly this raises the rate at ages 0–4 (from 47% to 70%) and 25–34 (from 18% to 26%) above the calculation where MDC 14 and 15 are omitted (Rate 2). Either way, the pattern is the same with very high rates of hospitalisation among infants, followed by a sharp decline among school age children, a shallow but steady rise thereafter to age 54, beyond which the rate of hospitalisation rises to almost 30 per cent among the aged.

As mentioned, individual patients may be hospitalised more than once, either for the same cause or for several separate causes. This results in separation rates that are much higher than unique patient-based hospitalisation rates. Using the same formula for calculating age-specific rates as outlined above, Figure 7.2 shows overall separation rates by broad age group. While the same pattern emerges, the distinguishing features are the noticeable effect of repeat hospital admissions among women of childbearing age, and, more strikingly, the very frequent hospital admissions among those aged over 45 years. Among these older people, the average patient is admitted to hospital 5.5 times.

Figure 7.2. Apparent age-specific separation rates: Aboriginal population of Thamarrurr region, 1998–2002[a]

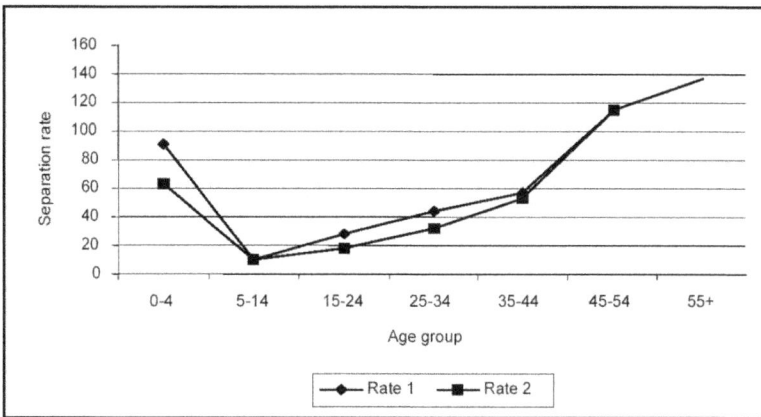

a.   Based on all recorded separations

Because of their somewhat distinct morbidity profiles, it is useful to consider the differences between males and females in terms of age-specific rates. However, the relatively small numbers in certain categories prevents the calculation of meaningful statistics. One alternative, then, is to observe the sex ratio (males as a proportion of females) among patients and separations at each age group. This is done in Table 7.3.

Table 7.3. Sex ratios of Aboriginal hospital patients and separations: Thamarrurr region residents, 1998–2002

Age (years)	Patients	Separations
0–4	1.16	1.13
5–14	1.21	1.36
15–24	0.19	0.11
25–34	0.33	0.19
35–44	0.28	0.11
45–54	0.35	0.05
55+	0.41	0.07
Total population	0.60	0.30

Source: NTDHCS, Darwin

There are more male patients and separations in the 0-4 age group, partly reflecting the higher sex ratio at birth, although this is even more so among the relatively few patients and separations that occur among school age children. From mid-teens onwards, however, females predominate. While the very low sex ratios between ages 15 and 44 partly reflect childbirth among women, there remain relatively few male patients, and even fewer separations at older ages beyond 45 years. Overall, the number of male patients is only two-thirds that of females, and the number of male separations only one-third that of female separations.

Hospitalisation diagnoses

In profiling the nature of morbidity as defined by principal disease diagnosis, data for all hospital separations (including repeat separations) are utilised. This is because individuals can, and often are, admitted to hospital more than once, but for quite different reasons. Accordingly, the distribution of cumulated Thamarrurr hospital patients and separations between 1998 and 2002 is shown by sex and MDC in Table 7.4. These are also illustrated in Figures 7.3 and 7.4 to assist interpretation.

Table 7.4. Distribution of Thamarrurr region hospital patients and separations by MDC and sex, 1998–2002

MDC	Patients			Separations		
	Males	Females	Total pop.	Males	Females	Total pop.
1	3.7	1.3	2.2	4.7	0.7	1.6
2	1.1	1.3	1.2	0.9	0.8	0.8
3	7.5	4.8	5.8	6.5	2.3	3.2
4	11.7	8.3	9.6	14.6	5.0	7.2
5	1.5	2.5	2.1	1.3	1.7	1.6
6	10.8	5.8	7.7	11.3	3.0	4.9
7	0.0	0.0	0.5	0.7	0.4	0.5
8	9.7	4.1	6.2	9.6	1.9	3.7
9	6.6	4.8	5.5	5.7	2.4	3.2
10	5.3	4.7	4.9	5.7	2.6	3.3
11	2.2	2.2	2.2	3.2	39.7	31.3
12	7.9	0.0	2.9	6.6	0.0	1.5
13	0.0	2.4	1.5	0.0	1.1	0.8
14	0.0	17.6	11.0	0.0	12.5	9.6
15	16.8	10.2	12.7	16.8	4.8	7.6
16	1.5	0.9	1.1	1.3	0.5	0.7
17	0.0	0.0	0.0	0.0	0.0	0.0
18	1.5	0.9	1.1	1.2	0.4	0.6
19	0.0	0.0	0.5	0.0	0.0	0.2
20	0.0	0.0	0.0	0.0	0.0	0.0
21	3.8	1.8	2.5	3.1	0.7	1.3
22	2.0	0.8	1.2	1.6	0.3	0.6
23	4.2	24.6	17.0	4.0	18.8	15.3
Total	100.0	100.0	100.0	100.0	100.0	100.0

Key to MDCs: 1. Nervous system; 2. Eye; 3. Ear, nose, mouth and throat; 4. Respiratory system; 5. Circulatory system; 6. Digestive system; 7. Hepatobilliary system and pancreas; 8. Musculoskeletal system and connective tissue; 9. Skin, subcutaneous tissue and breast; 10. Endocrine, nutritional & metabolic diseases and disorders; 11. Kidney and urinary tract; 12. Male reproductive system; 13. Female reproductive system; 14. Pregnancy, childbirth & the puerperium; 15. Newborns and other neonates; 16. Blood and blood-forming organs and immunological; 17. Neoplastic disorders; 18. Infectious & parasitic diseases; 19. Mental diseases and disorders; 20. Alcohol/drug use & alcohol/drug induced organic mental disorders; 21. Injuries, poisonings & toxic effects of drugs; 22. Burns; 23. Factors influencing health status & other contacts with health services.

Source: NTDHCS, Darwin

The first point to note is the quite distinct difference between male and female causes of hospitalisation. Almost one-fifth of separations among females were related to pregnancy and childbirth, while a similar proportion for males related to newborns and neonates. While concentration in these categories somewhat distorts comparison, it is still apparent that males and females have fairly different morbidity profiles. Thus, among males, diseases of the respiratory system, digestive system, and musculoskeletal system account for one third of all patients; among females, on the other hand, factors influencing health status and other contacts with health services (MDC 23) alone account for one-quarter of all patients. In line with the pattern across the Northern Territory, much of this contact with health services is haemodialysis treatment related to end-stage renal disease (ABS/AIHW 2003: 136–9). Some clue to this variation by sex is provided in Figure 7.4 which shows that separations among females for MDC 23 are four times higher as a share of all separations.

Figure 7.3. Distribution of Thamarrurr region hospital patients by MDC and sex, 1998–2002

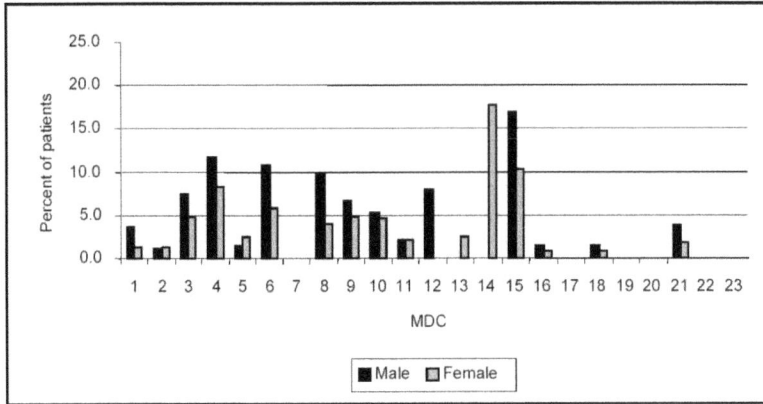

Key to MDCs: 1. Nervous system; 2. Eye; 3: Ear, nose, mouth and throat; 4. Respiratory system; 5. Circulatory system; 6. Digestive system; 7. Hepatobilliary system and pancreas; 8. Musculoskeletal system and connective tissue; 9. Skin, subcutaneous tissue and breast; 10. Endocrine, nutritional & metabolic diseases and disorders; 11. Kidney and urinary tract; 12. Male reproductive system; 13. Female reproductive system; 14. Pregnancy, childbirth & the puerperium; 15. Newborns and other neonates; 16. Blood and blood-forming organs and immunological; 17. Neoplastic disorders; 18. Infectious & parasitic diseases; 19. Mental diseases and disorders; 20. Alcohol/drug use & alcohol/drug induced organic mental disorders; 21. Injuries, poisonings & toxic effects of drugs; 22. Burns; 23. Factors influencing health status & other contacts with health services.

Source: NT DHCS, Darwin

Figure 7.4. Distribution of Thamarrurr region hospital separations by MDC and sex, 1998–2002

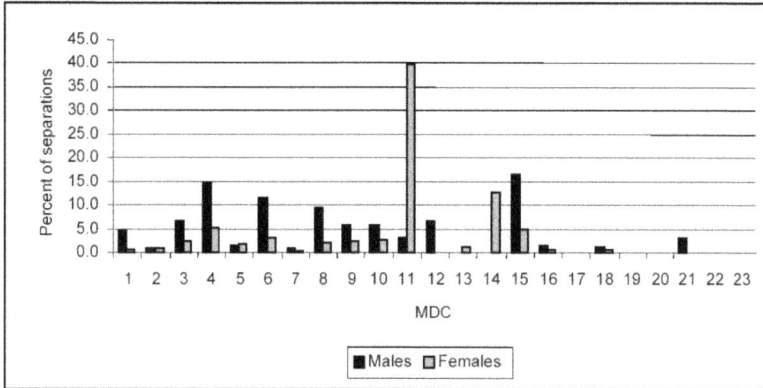

Key to MDCs: 1. Nervous system; 2. Eye; 3. Ear, nose, mouth and throat; 4. Respiratory system; 5. Circulatory system; 6. Digestive system; 7. Hepatobilliary system and pancreas; 8. Musculoskeletal system and connective tissue; 9. Skin, subcutaneous tissue and breast; 10. Endocrine, nutritional & metabolic diseases and disorders; 11. Kidney and urinary tract; 12. Male reproductive system; 13. Female reproductive system; 14. Pregnancy, childbirth & the puerperium; 15. Newborns and other neonates; 16. Blood and blood-forming organs and immunological; 17. Neoplastic disorders; 18. Infectious & parasitic diseases; 19. Mental diseases and disorders; 20. Alcohol/drug use & alcohol/drug induced organic mental disorders; 21. Injuries, poisonings & toxic effects of drugs; 22. Burns; 23. Factors influencing health status & other contacts with health services.

Source: NT DHCS, Darwin

Primary health status

Public domain data on the primary health status of Thamarrurr residents are limited. Although each active client of the Wadeye clinic has a clinical and medical record that provides essential background for health care delivery at the individual level, in terms of developing population health indicators such data are rarely aggregated for community-wide profiling. One notable exception is the reporting of chronic disease incidence via the Chronic Disease Register which is used by District Medical Officers on their visits to Wadeye. The purpose of the register is to provide a clinical summary of individual clients. Such data were provided by NTDHCS for June 2003 and the recorded instances of chronic disease are shown for males and females in Table 7.5.

This reveals many of the underlying chronic conditions that contribute to the morbidity statistics outlined above. Thus, diabetes and its associated conditions of renal disease, hypertension, hyperlipidemia, and coronary heart disease are most prevalent, along with rheumatic heart disease and chronic lung disease. In combination, these are indicative of past and current crowded living conditions, dietary patterns, and general lifestyle regimes. Of particular interest, though, is the degree to which chronic disease reporting is much higher for females as indicated by the very low sex ratios, especially for diabetes, early renal disease, asthma, and rheumatic heart disease. Reasons for this are unclear, especially given the context of higher adult male mortality, although this may indicate variable screening of the population.

Table 7.5. Notification of chronic diseases by sex: Wadeye clinic, June 2003

Disease	Males (1)	Females (2)	Total	Sex ratio (1/2)
Angina	*	*	5	*
AMI (heart attack)	*	*	7	*
Diabetes	19	49	68	0.39
IGT	*	10	12	*
Hypretension	61	55	116	1.11
Renal disease (early)	31	61	92	0.51
Renal disease (late)	*	*	10	*
Hyperlipedemia	10	12	22	0.83
Chronic lung disease	29	24	53	1.21
Asthma	19	32	51	0.59
Rheumatic fever	6	8	14	0.75
Rheumatic heart disease	12	41	53	0.29
Chronic liver disease	11	12	23	0.92
Schizophrenia	*	*	7	*
Epilepsy	7	*	10	*
Total	205	304	543	0.67

* indicates data suppressed for confidentiality

Source: NTDHCS, Darwin

Table 7.6 shows recorded instances of chronic diseases by broad age group and indicates the increase in reporting with age as well as the early onset of diabetes, renal, and rheumatic heart disease. On advice from NTDHCS, accurate calculation of the prevalence of chronic diseases is hampered by the uncertain extent and composition of population screening, by the lack of presentation of early symptoms (for example of angina), and by variable maintenance of the database. More fundamentally, many episodes of illness are not recognised at either the individual or household level and for that reason may not be presented for clinical assessment. With these limitations in mind, it nonetheless appears that chronic diseases are reported for somewhere in the region of one-quarter of the Thamarrurr population, with universal prevalence among the aged and affecting around two-thirds of those aged 35–54.

Child health

Many of the conditions that contribute to the overall profile of Aboriginal adult morbidity and mortality in the Thamarrurr region are likely to have their antecedents in poor childhood and maternal nutrition. Measures of weight and height gain provide a standard public health measure of poor nutrition by yielding estimates of children aged less than five years who are below average height for age (stunted), underweight for height (wasted), and below average weight for age (underweight). Levels of anaemia among those aged 6–9 months are also employed. These data are gathered as part of the NTDHCS Growth Assessment and Action (GAA) program and Table 7.7 shows the numbers of children reported for each of these characteristics against the total numbers measured at Wadeye clinic in 2002.

Table 7.6. Notification of chronic diseases by broad age group: Wadeye clinic, June 2003

MDC	<15	15–34	35–54	55+	Total
		Age (years)			
Angina	*	*	*	*	5
AMI (heart attack)	*	*	7	*	7
Diabetes	0	10	27	31	68
IGT	*	*	*	*	12
Hypertension	0	12	63	41	116
Renal disease (early)	0	15	52	25	92
Renal disease (late)	*	*	*	6	10
Hyperlipidemia	*	*	9	10	22
Chronic lung disease	*	*	11	35	53
Asthma	10	12	18	11	51
Rheumatic fever	*	9	*	*	14
Rheumatic heart disease	*	25	20	*	53
Chronic liver disease	*	12	*	*	23
Schizophrenia	*	*	*	*	7
Epilepsy	*	6	*	*	10
Total	10	101	207	159	543

*indicates data suppressed for confidentiality

Source: NTDHCS, Darwin

Table 7.7. Growth assessment of children aged less than five years: Wadeye clinic, 2002

Growth assessment	No. of children with the characteristic	Total measured	% of children measured	Coverage
Stunted	43	220	20.0	100.0
Underweight	47	220	21.0	100.0
Wasted	23	220	10.0	100.0
Anaemic[a]	8	184	4.0	98.0

a.   According to NTDHCS, an unknown proportion of the anaemia results in the GAA data set were post-treatment

Source: NTDHCS, Darwin

As shown, an estimated 20 per cent of children were found to be stunted, 21 per cent were underweight, and 10 per cent wasted. By comparison, the proportion anaemic was relatively low at four per cent, with population coverage of all relevant cohorts deemed to be comprehensive.

One further indicator of child health which is important as it reflects increased risk of neonatal and infant morbidity and mortality, is birthweight. This also reflects a number of preconditions including prematurity, poor maternal nutrition, high alcohol intake and smoking. Between 1997 and 2001, a total of 23 Aboriginal births to Thamarrurr mothers were recorded with a birthweight less than 2500 grams, out of a total of 200 live births. Thus, 11.5 per cent of births over this period were classified as low weight, which is slightly less than the figure of 13.6 per cent recorded for Aboriginal births in the Northern Territory as a whole between 1998 and 2000 (ABS/AIHW 2003: 126). It should be noted, however, that meaningful inter-regional comparison is compromised by the fact that the Thamarrurr rate is based on relatively few births and, in any case, there is potential undercount of births for designated communities such as Wadeye due to limitations in data recording.

Nutrition

It has long been recognised that poor diet and nutritional status are strongly associated (along with other risk factors) with a variety of chronic, preventable, and non-communicable diseases that are highly prevalent in Aboriginal communities. Primary among these in later life are cardiovascular disease and diabetes, but malnutrition also forms part of the general complex of reduced resistance to infectious and other disease and may engender its own morbidity profile. Not surprisingly, public health programs, especially those targeted at improving health outcomes among Aboriginal people, increasingly identify improved nutrition as an essential intervention. A prerequisite to successful intervention, however, is the identification of structural impediments to improved nutrition, many of which are behavioural and economic in nature, including patterns of household expenditure, store management, and food prices (Taylor & Westbury 2000).

As far as the last of these is concerned, the NTDHCS monitors supermarket, shop and community store food prices over time in order to establish price relativities in respect of a defined 'healthy basket' of goods. The monitoring device is the Community Market Basket Survey conducted annually. The survey was developed to ensure that the price of healthy foods was monitored; hence the focus on a standard 'healthy food basket' of 28 items. In addition to the price of goods, the quality and variety of selected food items is also established. By benchmarking these variables, the survey creates a capacity to assess changes in price, quality, and variety that may occur due to strategic interventions. It also allows for assessment of the capacity of community residents, given their incomes, to purchase a 'healthy basket' of food sufficient to feed a 'typical' family of six persons for 14 days. In the data provided by the NTDHCS, this assessment was based on an estimated fortnightly income from welfare payments of $1566 for this 'typical' family in 2002. This estimated income is set against the local cost of a healthy basket of food to establish the share of income required for its purchase.

The methodology employed in the surveys merits scrutiny because it affects the nature and scope of the data. The surveys are conducted annually and the data refer to a single day (usually in May of each year). Given the potential vagaries of store management and of food supply, the timing of each survey can thus be crucial in determining results. It should also be noted that if a price cannot be established for an item in the community store, then the town-based supermarket price is substituted: this may have the effect of deflating overall prices. No distinction is drawn between healthy and non-healthy takeaway foods, and the focus on healthy foods means that frequently purchased non-healthy items, such as carbonated soft drinks and potato chips, are not recorded. Finally, the data refer to the store at Wadeye, and so do not take into account the additional costs involved in purchasing food that is incurred by outstation residents.

With these limitations and biases in mind, the cost of purchasing components of a 'healthy basket of goods' at Wadeye in May 1999 is shown in Table 7.8, together with the district average for similar communities and for Darwin supermarkets. Overall in 2002, a total basket of food in Wadeye cost 10 per cent more than the District community average (as indicated by the ratio of the two prices at 109.7), and almost 40 per cent more than in Darwin supermarkets (ratio of 137.9). However, price relativities for different items in the healthy basket varied considerably, with the highest price gaps in 2002 recorded for bread and cereals and dairy foods. No items were cheaper in Wadeye compared to Darwin supermarkets, although Wadeye prices for fruits and vegetables were lower than the average for similar communities in the District.

Overall, the total cost of a healthy basket of goods at Wadeye per fortnight ($586) represents 37 per cent of the 'typical' family income, leaving just $980 for all other family requirements. With a total of 448 Centrepay deductions in Wadeye reported by Centrelink in April 2003, actual disposable income for most families in the region for remaining essentials such as clothing, transport, household and personal items, would be somewhat less than the $980 calculated above.

Table 7.8. Fresh food category by cost: Wadeye, Darwin and District stores, 2002

	Bread & cereals	Fruits	Vegetables	Meat, milk, eggs, cheese	Dairy foods	Other food	Total basket
	Comparison between Wadeye and district community						
Wadeye	$102	$124	$102	$98	$128	$32	$586
District community average	$83	$132	$112	$86	$95	$26	$534
Per cent difference	122%	0.94%	0.91%	114%	134.7%	123.0%	109.7%
	Comparison between Wadeye and Darwin supermarket						
Wadeye	$102	$124	$102	$98	$128	$32	$586
Darwin supermarket	$63	$121	$80	$68	$78	$14	$425
Per cent difference	161.9%	102.4%	127.5%	144.1%	164.1%	228.6%	137.9%

Source: NTDHCS, Darwin

A range of other data items are available from the Community Market Basket Survey including whether stores have a store management committee, or a food nutrition policy, the number of Aboriginal and non-Aboriginal workers employed at the store (six and 12 respectively at the Murrin-Patha Nimmipa store at Wadeye), the number of trainees and whether the store supports sporting and school activities as well as religious, cultural and funeral activities. Also indicated is the variety (different forms) and quality of individual fresh food groups—for example different types of vegetable, fruit and meats. Of the 15 food item categories surveyed, Wadeye store had a greater number of choices available than the district average in seven categories, and had less choice in four categories (low sugar canned fruit, frozen vegetables, dried vegetables, canned fish), although some of this difference may reflect that fact that far greater choice of fresh fruit and vegetables was available at Wadeye. As for the quality of fresh food items, out of 39 fruit and vegetable items, only three were considered of 'poor' quality, four items were 'fair', and the vast majority (32) was classified as 'good'. As for the availability of healthy foods other than fresh foods (baby foods, oils, margarine, milk, legumes, and other foods), 80 per cent of the 24 items listed for survey were available at Wadeye store.

Health-related quality of life assessment

The extent to which policy interventions are perceived by individuals to effect an improvement in their quality of life is an emergent concern of health policy in Australia, including in regard to Aboriginal people (Brady, Kunitz & Nash 1997). This concern with measures of health status that go beyond objective indicators such as morbidity and mortality is based on the recognition that a full assessment of health status should include physical, mental, social, and spiritual dimensions.

A more practical reason is the need for timely assessment of health interventions which may take a long time to translate into changes in conventional indicators of health status, such as those compiled using hospitals separations data, especially at the whole-of-population level. Furthermore, it appears that many health treatments, while effective from a biomedical point of view, may actually compromise quality of life. An example is the treatment of end-stage renal disease, which requires the relocation of rural-based patients into Darwin for dialysis with attendant difficulties in sustaining the comfort and care provided by family members. Individuals also have to adjust to living in an unfamiliar and institutional environment and financial hardships can be incurred, especially in terms of the wider caring responsibilities of family groups. All these factors can make treatment costly in terms of loss of quality of life, and may make non-compliance (and associated shortened life expectancy) preferable to adherence (Willis 1995).

A number of standard instruments have been developed in an attempt to discover individuals' perceptions of their own health-related quality of life (QOL). These can be repeated over time to monitor changes in condition, and produce results that are comparable with other groups. They cover a number of QOL-related aspects of health, such as physical functioning, emotional well-being and support from family. Some of these instruments, such as the question on self-assessed health status within the main sample of National Health Survey (NHS), are regularly used in Australia and are considered to be reliable, valid, and responsive to changes in clinical condition. While this conclusion has been drawn for Aboriginal people in urban settings, the same cannot be claimed for data from remote communities where mainstream conceptions of quality of life and links to health status are indeterminate and poorly understood (ABS/National Centre for Epidemiology and Population Health (NCEPH) 1997; Senior 2003).

As far as the Thamarrurr region is concerned such population-based assessments are non-existent, although to the extent that Thamarrurr residents participated in the 1994 National Aboriginal and Torres Strait Islander Survey (NATSIS), their responses to the standard global question, 'In general, would you say that your health is excellent, very good, good, fair or poor?' would be subsumed with the responses for the Jabiru ATSIC Region as a whole. In this much wider region, as with elsewhere in remote Australia, answers to this question appeared somewhat counter-intuitive. For example, although 33 per cent of respondents reported an illness in the two weeks prior to the survey, and 22 per cent reported one or more long-term illness, 98 per cent considered themselves to be in very good or excellent health, while just one per cent described their health as being poor (ABS 1996a: 17–19). Although this raises an obvious question of why people rate their health as good or excellent when the statistics show it to be otherwise, no research is available to provide an answer.

Primary health care services

One factor that has been identified as influential in determining health outcomes is the degree of access to primary health care services. Planning for such access in the Thamarrurr region falls within another new but wider regional structure in the form of the Top End West Primary Health Care Access Planning (PHCAP) zone. Within this framework, levels of primary health care service resources were estimated for the Top End Regional Indigenous Health Planning Committee of the Northern Territory Aboriginal Health Forum in 2000 (Bartlett & Duncan 2000). This exercise aimed to establish measures of access to health services based on the notion of an ideal staff to service population ratio for Aboriginal health workers (AHWs), nurses and doctors. The results for each community in the Northern Territory were then ranked to provide a relative measure of staffing needs. With some accommodation for economies of scale, the ideal staffing ratios adopted were one AHW for every 50 people, one nurse for every 200 people, and one doctor for every 400 people. On the author's own admission, this formula provides a very basic assessment of staffing needs using quite limited parameters (Bartlett & Duncan 2000: 37). However, it did suggest that in 2000, Wadeye performed rather poorly relative to many other localities as it was ranked 33rd out of 49 communities in terms of the adequacy of its health staff resources (Bartlett & Duncan 2000: 204).

Table 7.9 shows the actual staffing situation at Wadeye clinic in June 2003. Overall, 11 personnel were employed, although this amounted to only eight full-time equivalent positions, two of which were non-medical. The most striking feature for a population centre that is set to exceed the size of present-day Nhulunbuy within a generation, is the continuing lack of a resident doctor.

Table 7.9. Staff by stream and Indigenous status: Wadeye clinic, June 2003

	Full-time equivalent			Head count		
	Indigenous	Non-Indigenous	Total	Indigenous	Non-Indigenous	Total
Administrative	1.0	0.0	1.0	1	0	1
AHW	1.9	0.0	1.9	5	0	5
Nursing	0.0	4.0	4.0	0	4	4
Physical	1.0	0.0	1.0	1	0	1
Total	3.9	4.0	7.9	7	4	11

Source: NTDHCS, Darwin

8. Regional involvement in the criminal justice system

According to the 1994 NATSIS, an estimated 19 per cent of Aboriginal people aged 13 years and over in the Jabiru ATSIC Region had been arrested by police in the previous five years (ABS 1996a: 56). This was very close to the average of 20 per cent reported for the Northern Territory as a whole. At the same time, according to the Wadeye Community Youth Support Management Group, Wadeye has the highest per capita juvenile offending rate in the Northern Territory with young people from Wadeye constituting a significant proportion of all those in detention. Clearly, interaction with the police, and then subsequently with the courts, custodial institutions, and diversionary programs is commonplace in the lives of Aboriginal individuals and families in the region, as well as those associated with them. While recidivism in the Thamarrurr region is frequently portrayed as providing a measure of social dysfunction, precisely how dysfunction might be defined and explained in this particular cultural setting is only just beginning to be understood, although it is clear that the issues are more complex and culturally bound than a simple model of low socio-economic status leading to social dysfunction would suggest (Ivory 2003). One line of argument suggests that by deliberately seeking incarceration via their actions Aboriginal youth are engaging in an alternative rite of passage to manhood (Biles 1983), although Ogilvie and Van Zyl (2001) view detention not as a rite of passage but rather as simply another venue for the construction of identity among marginalised and bored adolescents who are desperate for change to their routine.

Whatever the underlying causes, for the purpose of profiling, recidivism is viewed here in its literal sense as simply the extent to which individuals repeatedly transgress the criminal code. Having said that, one relationship between crime rates and the regional society and economy that is reasonably apparent concerns the degree to which past and present convictions and interaction with police, courts and prisons, influence individual chances of participating successfully in the regional society and economy. By presenting select summary statistics from police records, court records and correctional services records for residents of the Thamarrurr region (to the extent that this is possible) this chapter will attempt to derive estimates of the population for whom contact with the police and a criminal conviction might represent a barrier, or at least a brake, on social and economic participation (Hunter & Borland 1999). Along the way, some sense of the nature of criminal activity and its implied impact on the social fabric will also be provided.

Data sources

Crime statistics for the Thamarrurr region are available from a variety of sources reflecting different stages of interaction with the criminal justice system. The initiating factor, of course, is contact with the police either by way of reporting a crime or via an apprehension (arrest), or summons. Such actions yield a range of data concerning the nature of offences and offenders with separate reporting for juveniles and adults. Individuals who are charged with an offence are further processed by the courts (a charge being an allegation laid by the police before the court or other prosecuting agency that a person has committed a criminal offence). Statistics relating to the activities of the Supreme Court are captured by the Northern Territory Department of Justice Statistical Summary. As for those charged who are found guilty of an offence, data are provided by Correctional Services, while non-custodial community corrections data are available from the records of the Juvenile Diversion Division of the Northern Territory Police.

Reported offences

Contact between the police and the regional population is recorded as persons are apprehended by the police (either via arrest or summons), or are diverted (as juveniles) through the cautioning system and referred to the Juvenile Diversion Division. Data on offences reported in this way at Wadeye, including all reported offences for which no offenders were apprehended, are shown in Table 8.1 for 2002. A total of 329 offences were reported, one third of which involved property damage, 29 per cent involved assault, 18 per cent were for unlawful entry into dwellings and businesses, with a similar proportion for motor vehicle and other theft. It should be noted, of course, that these are reported offences—not reported offenders with the latter almost certainly far fewer in number.

Table 8.1. Reported offences by category: Wadeye, 2002

Offence category	No. reported	% of all offences
Assault	89	27.5
Sexual assault	4	1.2
Other against the person	2	0.6
Unlawful entry – dwelling	23	7.1
Unlawful entry – business	33	10.2
Motor vehicle theft	13	4.0
Other theft	46	14.2
Property damage	111	34.3
Other property offences	3	0.9
Total	324	100.0

Source: Northern Territory Office of Crime Prevention, Darwin

Correctional services

The findings of court proceedings in the form of penalties (sentences) can be grouped into four broad categories: custodial, non-custodial, fines and dismissals. According to the ABS sentence type classification (ABS 2003: 71), custodial orders involve custody in a correctional institution as life imprisonment, imprisonment with a determined term, or periodic detention, with the latter applying only to juveniles. Non-custodial orders include a variety of community supervision or work orders and community service orders, as well as probation and treatment orders. Other non-custodial orders include good behaviour bonds and recognisance orders, while monetary orders basically refer to fines or recompense to victims as well as licence disqualification/suspension/amendment and forfeiture of property.

In 2001/02, a total of 193 matters were lodged at the court of summary jurisdiction at Wadeye, with 133 finalised in the same year. In the juvenile court, 27 matters were lodged in 2001/02, and 35 were finalised. An indication of the outcomes of these hearings is provided by data from correctional services on prisoners, juvenile detention and conditional liberty orders.

Custodial sentences

In the Northern Territory census of prisoners in June 2002, a total of 32 Indigenous prisoners indicated Wadeye as their last known address. All of these were males. Because this number is relatively small, it is necessary to use data from several censuses in order to disaggregate select sentencing and social characteristics. Thus, between 2000 and 2002, a total of 79 prisoners indicated Wadeye as their usual address. Of these, 48 per cent were imprisoned for assault, 18 per cent for break and enter and property damage, and 10 per cent for motor vehicle offences. The length of sentence varied considerably with 15 per cent of sentences for less than six months, 19 per cent between six months and one year, 29 per cent between one and five years, and 15 per cent over five years. One-fifth of Wadeye prisoners were on remand. As for the age of prisoners, 15 per cent were aged between 18 and 19 years, 57 per cent were between 20 and 29 years, 20 per cent were between 30 and 39 years, and eight per cent were aged between 40 and 49 years. Using the single-year age data that underlie Table 2.3, together with prison census data for 2002, some idea of the imprisonment rate among Wadeye males in different age groups can be established. This is shown in Figure 8.1.

Figure 8.1. Imprisonment rate by age: Wadeye males, 30 June 2002

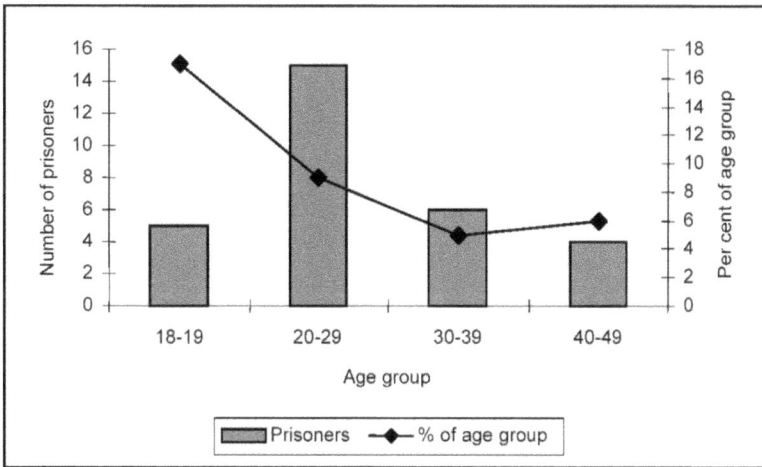

Source: Northern Territory Office of Crime Prevention, Darwin

Thus, a total of five Wadeye males aged 18 and 19 were imprisoned, and while this seems a relatively small number it nonetheless represents 16 per cent of that age group. The largest number of prisoners were aged between 20 and 29 years, although as Figure 8.1

shows the rate of imprisonment declines with age. Partly because of this, almost two-thirds of those imprisoned (62%) were single men.

Using the three years of data for 2000–2002, it is significant to note that the vast majority (91%) of Wadeye prisoners had previous experience in correctional centres suggesting that the data reflect a core group of repeat offenders. As to clues regarding their socio-economic status, the educational background is consistent with that profiled for Wadeye males as a whole in Chapter 5. Thus, the majority (46%) had primary level schooling only, 37 per cent had some secondary level schooling, four per cent had completed secondary level, and 11 per cent had post secondary education which probably reflects their participation in TAFE training courses. In a few cases, no formal schooling was indicated. In turn, these education levels are manifest in labour force status with two-thirds (67%) of prisoners previously unemployed, and only 23 per cent employed.

Juvenile diversion

In 2001/02, a total of 10 juveniles from Wadeye aged between 13 and 17 commenced a detention episode in a correctional centre. Since 2000, however, the aim of policy has been to divert juveniles (those under 18), away from the formal justice and courts system except in cases where serious offences are committed or where options to prevent re-offending have proven unsuccessful. The guiding principles are to support and involve victims, and to encourage parental responsibility and community involvement in reducing youth crime. Diversionary conferencing is the key management tool for this purpose, and this involves police, families, and the community jointly determining the nature of amends to be made for harm done with rehabilitation as the prime aim.

In 2002/03, a total of 123 juvenile apprehensions were recorded in Wadeye District. Most of these apprehensions (70 per cent) were for unlawful entry, primarily into buildings, although a few (eight) involved entry into dwellings. The next largest offence type was unlawful use of motor vehicles (15%). For the most part, it was male youths who were apprehended with only three females recorded, and the majority of these (81%) were aged between 15 and 17 years, although this means that 19 per cent were aged 14 years. In processing these apprehensions, a total of 37 individuals (31%) were offered diversion from the courts system, which meant that by far the majority (69%) were dealt with by the courts.

Family conferencing was the most common method of handling diversion referrals with this strategy applied in 67 per cent of cases. Victim/offender conferencing was applied in 24 per cent of cases. In three instances a written warning was issued. At this stage, diversion case management and program support is embryonic—in 2002/03, 27 case management events were recorded, but only six individuals were engaged in formal diversionary programs. With regard to the latter, the aim of the Wadeye Youth Development Working Group is to develop personal and family action plans that would include a range of requirements such as attendance at Kardu Kigay, work experience with CDEP, attendance at drug and alcohol sessions, cultural activities, practical life skills, arts, and team sports. Ironically, one measure of success in regard to juvenile crime at Wadeye would be a rise over time in the numbers recorded in diversionary programs.

9. Implications for regional planning

The purpose of this analysis has been to portray the social and economic status of the population resident within the Thamarrurr Regional Council area at the commencement of initiatives resulting from new arrangements for regional governance. The value of such a profile is twofold. First, it assists in providing a quantum to discussions of need, aspirations, and regional development capacities. Second, it creates a benchmark against which the impact of any developmental decisions and future actions associated with them may be measured. Thus, the content of this report provides the basis for a dialogue in regional planning, as well as the means to measure aspects of its impact. With this in mind, the key implications of findings in regard to each of the baseline indicators presented are summarised below.

Demography

Contrary to the situation of population decline and ageing that constitutes the 'regional problem' for many parts of agricultural Australia, the 'problem' in the Thamarrurr region is how to accommodate growth and a burgeoning youthful profile. This is an expanding population with high growth momentum, that is committed to country (undeniably mobile, but not overtly migrant), and which is likely to produce the Territory's fourth largest town within a generation. From the time of their first contact with non-Aboriginal people in the mid-nineteenth century, but especially since Catholic missionaries arrived to settle in the 1930s, Aboriginal peoples of the region have experienced significant demographic change involving the concentration of previously dispersed population groups into the town of Wadeye and substantial growth in population numbers due mostly to natural increase. This recent phase of high population growth coincides first of all with the integration of Aboriginal people into mission life, and more recently, with the extension of citizen entitlements and related expansion of service provision in the region, notably in areas of health and social security.

As for the non-Aboriginal residents, their numbers have increased since the days of mission control although they remain fairly steady as a share of the regional population (around five per cent) given the direct link between non-Aboriginal residence and skilled employment mostly in administration and the provision of essential services. If one of the development impacts in coming years is an expansion of economic activity and service provision requiring further skilled labour, one effect that the Thamarrurr Region Council will need to consider is the possibility that this will lead to an increase in the non-Aboriginal population of the region.

While the Thamarrurr population can be geographically defined, it is in no way socially bound, with family, social and economic links to all surrounding regions. Already, a floating population from this extended pool adds to the numbers resident in the region at any one time and results in additional loads placed on services, notably housing. To the extent that this short-term movement into and out of the Thamarrurr region is a response to a perceived balance of opportunities and constraints (pushes and pulls) between different localities across a much wider Top End social and economic network, the potential for developments at Thamarrurr to alter the balance of regional place utility in its own favour may serve to increase service population loads. Examples here might include an upgrading of the school to secondary status, improved housing availability, or successful economic development leading to job creation.

The overriding demographic characteristic is high Aboriginal fertility leading to sustained rapid population growth and a high proportion of infants and children. This will lead to an almost doubling of the Aboriginal population within a generation with high potential for continued growth beyond that. However, the big unknown in this demographic equation remains net migration, although it does appear that individuals born within the region conduct their affairs and pass through life mostly *in situ*. This demographic stability reflects, in part, the strength of cultural continuity and a desire and growing capacity to sustain chosen lifestyles on country. But an untested and important question is the extent to which it also reflects an incapacity to engage wider social and economic structures for want of adequate human capital.

While the projections of population are correct according to the algorithms applied, they provide only a possible scenario. One device frequently deployed for planning purposes is to canvass a range of possible outcomes based on varying assumptions. An obvious further development, then, would be the generation of alternative scenarios based on possible combinations of falling, rising or stable fertility and mortality and varying assumptions about net migration. While there is some exploratory potential here in providing answers to *what if* questions, this should be based on plausible assumptions. Just as an example, if the TFR in the present projection was allowed to decline by one per cent per annum, and all other projection assumptions remained intact, then the regional population by 2023 would be noticeably lower at 3564, while the base of the age pyramid would be less pronounced with much reduced population momentum. Such a scenario is entirely feasible. Indeed an even more substantial reduction in future population growth could easily be envisaged if, for example, wholesale use of fertility control technology were to be adopted, in particular female contraception (information on the prevalence of family planning is not easily acquired, and so the extent to which current fertility might already be controlled by such methods is difficult to assess). In such a situation the effects of reduced fertility would substantially impact on future numbers with planning consequences quite different from those implied by the present set of figures. Thus, an abiding feature of population projections is the stimulus they provide for debate on the future demographic outcomes of particular social and economic behaviours. As such, they enable community discussion about alternate paths to regional objectives.

Local interest in such matters of demography is clearly evident. Because of concerns regarding the accuracy of official population figures, a highly significant step in developing baseline demographic data was the decision by the Thamarrurr Region Council to organise to count its own people. A key to the success of this count was the use of locally generated population lists as a cross-check against individuals recorded at dwellings—a device that has been demonstrated elsewhere to enhance population coverage (Martin and Taylor

1996). As a consequence, Thamarrurr Council now has a baseline demographic database of the usual residents of its region, plus an estimate of the regional service population, with which to consider the size of current and future needs. This process was an important exercise in capacity building for governance as it involved key local people in collecting and verifying their own population data to be used for their own purposes. No longer do Canberra or Darwin tell Thamarrurr who they are, Thamarrurr tells them!

Jobs and economic status

Against the stated aims of key Commonwealth and Territory policy initiatives, it is clear that economic outcomes for Aboriginal people in the Thamarrurr region are way below optimal. Less than one-fifth of all adults are currently employed, and the vast majority of these are tied to CDEP. Aboriginal people occupy fewer than half of the 130 or so jobs outside of CDEP. The result is that 82 per cent of Aboriginal income is sourced from welfare payments. Of the estimated $4 million in personal income from mainstream employment, only 16 per cent of this goes to Aboriginal employees. Viewed historically, it is likely that Aboriginal people are less inclined now to be participating in the workforce than in previous generations. Of particular concern is the fact that 45 per cent of those who are not in the workforce, and 35 per cent of the unemployed, are in the 15–24 age group.

The scale of job creation required to make an impact on this labour force status is very substantial as the working age population is set to expand rapidly. Just to maintain the current very low employment rate will require a doubling of those in work over the next 20 years. Even if Aboriginal people were to occupy every job in Thamarrurr, at current levels this would be far too few to make inroads. Either way, though, cheap policy options appear unavailable—resources will either be needed for remedial action to enhance education, training and job creation, otherwise the costs of welfare and management of social pathologies due to business as usual will escalate. Whatever the case, a fiscal response is unavoidable.

The other clear message is that the majority of adults are likely to be unemployed or outside the official workforce into the foreseeable future. This is especially so if the whole adult population is seen as eligible. However, given the focus in the Thamarrurr Agreement on youth and children, improvement in measurable employment outcomes would be made more achievable by targeting particular cohorts for attention. In this regard, the present low participation rate in the school-to-work transition years is striking, and any attempt to enhance future employment outcomes would need to address the general level of readiness for work.

In the meantime, employment generation is most likely to occur via an import substitution model embracing activities such as the construction and maintenance of housing and physical infrastructure (including roads), education, health services, retailing, public administration and planning, transport, media, land restoration, land management, and tourism. Some of the diversity in economic activity encompassed here is already in place via CDEP schemes, although it is rarely recognised as such, often being seen amorphously as 'just' CDEP work. The degree to which this represents cost-shifting and substitution for proper Commonwealth, Territory and local government funding of employment in the provision of essential services needs to be examined and addressed.

Presently, imported non-Aboriginal workers occupy many regionally based jobs, as they tend to be managerial, professional and trade positions requiring particular skills and job-readiness. While there is unlikely to be rapid 'Indigenisation' of such positions, the system of mentoring local middle managers in many occupations is an important first step. Alongside this, there is a parallel need to tackle deeper structural hurdles if local people are to successfully compete for skilled mainstream jobs with potential in-migrants, both Aboriginal and non-Aboriginal. These include the minimal numbers who progress to secondary level education with requisite literacy and numeracy skills, which in part reflects low school participation and attendance levels, as well as relatively low participation and successful completion in post-school, certificate level training courses.

However, even if local people occupied all such positions, there would remain a large deficit in numbers employed according to projections of working age population. Thus, the real planning need is to explore ways of generating labour-intensive economic activity which, in the particular cultural setting of Thamarrurr, places an emphasis on strengthening elements of customary economic activity as epitomised, for example, by the Thamarrurr Rangers program, and as manifest in the widespread production of arts and crafts. Since 1997, as many as 126 local artists have sold works via the Dirrmu Ngakumarl gallery, and while only a handful remain associated, and fewer still have received significant economic return, the potential for enhancing economic activity in the industry is nonetheless clear, as recognised by the Northern Territory government's Indigenous Arts Strategy (Altman 2003; Northern Territory Government 2003b).

Also significant here are the Thamarrurr Regional Council's plans for the development of local employment opportunities based on the establishment of a regional construction industry. The basis for this industry planning lies in the substantial existing backlog of regional housing and infrastructure need, as well as the expanding requirements to accommodate population growth and provide maintenance services. Notwithstanding keen interest, one difficulty that communities experience in converting such economic opportunities into local employment is their inevitably higher cost structure in competitive tendering with urban-based contractors. To the extent that this is an issue at Thamarrurr, the 'whole of government' partnership that forms the basis of the COAG ICCP trial provides a potentially unique framework to consider the opportunity costs of government tendering processes in terms of the social consequences and dollar costs of foregone regional employment. In effect, the lowest tender for public works may not necessarily present the cheapest option for government overall.

Education and training

Poor employment outcomes for Aboriginal people in the region are to a large degree tied to poor educational status. It remains the case that not all of those in the current school age group are enrolled. Only half of the region's school age population is enrolled at school, and only half of those enrolled actually attend classes, and even then often on an irregular basis. The low level of commitment to school attendance in the region is reflected in minimal retention to post-primary years with less than one-fifth of teenagers of compulsory school age estimated to be attending classes. In effect, only a handful of school leavers enter working age with high school level achievement and skills.

Likewise, the very low participation in Certificate level VET courses means that the vast majority of Aboriginal adults in the region are likely to be left uneducated, unqualified, unemployed, or underemployed on CDEP, and effectively marginalised in the face of any competition for jobs from more qualified countrymen or outsiders. Thus, a key regional development challenge is going to be in ensuring equitable, not just partial participation. Having said that, even qualified local people are underemployed, with many holding Certificate level qualifications that have never been practically applied. One glaring example concerns the 27 Wadeye residents who achieved level II certification from the Northern Territory University in Tourism (site guides) in 1999. The aim was to prepare a workforce for a tourism venture that never materialised. This underlines the case that skills development needs to be closely tied to the creation of employment opportunities.

Housing and infrastructure

By Territory standards, Wadeye is a settlement of significant size. Within a generation it will be larger than present-day Nhulunbuy. Despite this, it fails to match the levels of infrastructure development and housing adequacy that are normally associated with Australian settlements of equivalent size. With housing for Aboriginal residents provided initially by the mission, and now by the Council, supply is entirely program driven and falls far short of demand. As with employment, the backlog is such that a substantial increase in stock will be required simply to prevent the current high levels of overcrowding from being exacerbated.

Currently, the Northern Territory government estimates the cost of meeting agreed standards in housing for the Thamarrurr region at $52 million, based on an average bedroom cost of $60 000. In addition to this is a need to ensure that adequate maintenance funds are available and sufficient to ensure minimum environmental health standards, while expansion in the housing stock will be necessary to accommodate new household formation in a rapidly growing population.

While the available data provide some basis for estimating housing needs, more precise information is required on the functionality of dwellings in terms of environmental health infrastructure, and there is a need to better understand the load on housing stock created by short-term mobility into and within the region. At a more general level, it would be useful to draw comparison between Wadeye and other Australian towns of comparable size and growth rate to establish the degree of difference in infrastructure and approaches to physical planning for growth.

Health status

With reference to just one statistic—mean age at death (which currently stands at 46 years for Aboriginal people in the Daly SLA)—the physical limitations on prolonged and full participation in the workforce become all too apparent. If we add to this the fact of relatively high morbidity rates commencing in the mid-30s and rising throughout the prime working ages, then a pattern emerges of severe physical constraints on the ability of many in the community to engage in meaningful and sustained economic activity. From a labour market perspective, the extent to which poor health status impacts on the workforce participants would be better understood if data were available on any links between health status and below average school performance. There is also the likelihood that less direct impacts on workforce participation might exist, such as individuals not seeking work due to responsibilities in caring for sick relatives.

Among the issues underlying health status, the profile emphasises the significance of ongoing backlogs in achieving adequate environmental health infrastructure (including a reduction in overcrowded dwellings), a continuing gap between ideal and actual staffing levels in health personnel, and difficulties in achieving better nutritional status in the population given the high cost of food and low incomes. One of the key health issues for the future is the distinct prospect that overall morbidity and chronic disease levels will rise in line with growing numbers in older age groups. While health status generally reflects prevailing social and economic conditions in the region, there is an inevitable lag between any improvement in the latter and its possible effect on the former. This lag will be further prolonged by the expansion of older age groups.

Criminal justice

A pressing issue for Thamarrurr is the degree to which past and present convictions and interaction with police, courts and prisons influence individual chances of participating successfully in the regional society and economy as defined by the goals and objectives of the ICCP partners. While limited by data availability, an estimate is provided here of the population for whom contact with the police and a criminal conviction might represent a barrier, or at least a brake, on social and economic participation. What emerges is a picture of some 10 per cent of adults aged under 30 (almost all male) who are in custody at any one time. Many of these are repeat offenders, and while custody rates decline with age, feeding into this group is a larger number of juvenile offenders and even more children of primary school age who essentially experience an apprehension-free apprenticeship into recidivist behaviour. Not that sanction by the criminal justice system appears to matter much as a deterrent, indeed it may even be sought.

The main thrust of research into underlying causes of such behaviour among Aboriginal youth in remote communities emphasises the futility of custody in circumstances where the normal progression from school to paid work is the exception rather than the rule (Ogilvie & Van Zyl 2001). While the educational profile of offenders recorded in official crime statistics appears to be in line with the general Thamarrurr profile, one can't help but postulate at least some link between the lack of participation in schooling observed in the region, the low level of youth labour force participation, and the scale of youth participation in recidivist activity.

As Ogilvie and Van Zyl (2001: 4) point out, if an individual's most defining experience of growing up is primarily about custody, (and one might add gang allegiance in the case of Wadeye), then it would seem unlikely that such an experience would equip young males for lives outside of criminal subcultures. In pursuing this theme, they call for a reconsideration of expenditure involved in incarceration in favour of facilitating less destructive modes of growing up (Ogilvie & Van Zyl 2001: 5). To this extent, continued poor school attendance and failure to engage youth economically 'to satisfy the need for more than just boredom and marginalisation' (Ogilvie and Van Zyl 2001: 5), represent clear opportunity costs to both government and the regional community.

Information systems for regional planning

In order to maximise the positives from regional governance, it is central that any consequences of development should be managed rather than arbitrary. A fundamental step in establishing mechanisms for the management of development processes is the construction of a baseline profile of social and economic conditions at the outset. Without this, it is difficult to determine the subsequent effects of one course of action over any other. Accordingly, this need to measure outcomes from a baseline is fundamental to development plans negotiated between government and regional governing bodies.

As an example of this, the Shared Responsibility Agreement signed in 2003 between the Thamarrurr Regional Council, the Northern Territory Government, and the Commonwealth, identifies as its first objective 'the establishment of partnerships for achieving measurable and sustainable improvements for people living in the region.' The measures required to inform both Thamarrurr and government about progress were determined partly by the development priorities set out within the Thamarrurr Agreement, and partly by the availability of public information specific to the regional population.

While by their very nature, baseline data are cross-sectional, the projection of the regional population to 2023 (a generation from now) encourages forward thinking and anticipation of needs so as to hopefully respond to them before they are realized. This capacity to project future population levels is an essential adjunct to the preparation of baseline data. All too often in Indigenous Affairs, policy has been 'reactive' by responding to historic levels of need thereby creating a constant sense of catch up. What is required for good governance is a 'proactive' methodology that seeks to anticipate and plan for expected requirements. In this way, the content and intent of regional agreements with government can be translated into a required quantum of program and partner commitments over a given time frame. This issue of future needs leads naturally to a discussion of capacity building for regional governance.

Partnerships and capacity building

The process of developing a baseline profile of the Thamarrurr regional population involved a large number of agencies and individuals from Wadeye itself, and from Territory and Commonwealth agencies. Regional data for a customised area such as Thamarrurr are not readily available; they need to be requested, even cajoled, from a variety of sources and then locally interpreted. Aside from ABS census data, other indicators to do with welfare, income, housing, employment, education, health, crime, and even demography, have to be constructed with assistance from line agencies.

Thus, an early test of the partnership arrangement in the context of developing the baseline profile was the extent to which Commonwealth, Territory, and local community agencies could, and did, deliver on access to relevant data to support the construction of social indicators. In the Thamarrurr exercise, an important first step in accessing these data was the bringing together of all relevant Commonwealth and Territory agencies to a common meeting to discuss and negotiate the means by which this would occur. Although much can be promised at such gatherings, the speed of response can be variable and considerable follow up is necessary. As seen from the data list, administrative and public domain information is largely restricted to aggregate region-level data.

The emphasis in the Thamarrurr Agreement on evidence-based outcomes underlines the need for accurate demographic data. Whatever the detail of regional plans, it is crucial that these are based on reliable estimates of the population they are intended for. Globally, this requires reliable totals. Program-wise, it requires reliable breakdown into infants, mothers, school age children, youth, young adults, middle-aged, and older people. Culture-wise, it requires social mapping into groups that have local significance such as age grades, family groups and clans.

In Thamarrurr, the basis for an accurate count of the population was established by the Regional Council itself, working with the various groups established within the Thamarrurr governance structure to address priority issues. Of particular note here were the Thamarrurr Regional Housing Authority, and the Palngun Wurnangat Womens Association. This process alone was an exercise in capacity building for governance as it involved key local people in collecting and verifying their own population data to be used for their own purposes.

The outcome is a database that enables the Regional Council to consider options and needs for the future. With this information, the Council now knows that just to achieve a very modest goal and keep the regional employment rate at its current very low level (14%), the number of adults in work will need to double over the next 20 years. Also, with the school age population rising to well over 1000 within a generation, there is a strong case for upgrading the school to secondary status. As for health issues, the fact that older age groups are likely to increase fastest over the next 20 years has substantial implications for health spending and provision of facilities in the region, given the age profile and nature of morbidity. Finally, in planning to address housing needs, substantial additional resourcing is going to be needed just to sustain the current regional occupancy rate at 16 persons per functional dwelling, let alone reduce it.

For effective planning it is essential that the information system constructed to inform regional governance should be ongoing, constantly updated, and expanded where necessary. Aside from the ability to establish region-wide needs, the database developed for Thamarrurr can be further developed by configuring it into family/clan groups, while additional information such as housing, jobs, and education can also be grafted on to suit the needs of the various ICCP priority working groups. Accordingly, this task should be seen as a core function within the regional governance structure. Indeed, it could be argued that one measure of success in terms of establishing good governance, is that regional councils, such as Thamarrurr, begin to assume responsibility for the compilation of their own indicators (in partnership with government agencies who often hold the necessary data), and to progress in stages to their interpretation, presentation, replication, and dissemination with the ultimate goal of their application for planning. What is presented in the current profile is akin to the rapid appraisal approach to social and economic profiling with associated shortcomings as described by Birckhead (1999). For the next phase in the development of regional information systems, more appropriate models should involve enhanced community participation and various approaches to this exist (Howitt 1993; Josif & Associates 1995a, 1995b, 1995c; Walsh & Mitchell 2002).

In particular, agencies faced with imperfect data for development planning have moved to establish demographic surveillance systems at various sites across the developing world (Binka et al. 1999; IDRC 2002). These now provide an internationally recognised set of tools, methods, procedures and guidelines for the successful tracking of regional population dynamics and measurement of intervention impacts that would bear useful replication in the Thamarrurr context.

As with many aspects of Indigenous life, information gathering and interpretation tends to be presently done *for* communities *by* outsiders. With appropriate resourcing, training and skills development for local personnel, the ICCP trials represent a unique opportunity to build internal regional capacity for planning within the framework of associated emerging governance structures. This sense of ownership and participation in the planning process, and the information flow that informs it, is central to good governance and community development.

References

Aboriginal and Torres Strait Islander Commission (ATSIC) 1994, *The National Aboriginal Health Strategy: An Evaluation*, ATSIC, Canberra.

Akerman, K. 1979, 'Material culture and trade in the Kimberleys today', in R. M. Berndt and C. H. Berndt (eds), *Aborigines of the West: Their Past and Their Present*, University of Western Australia Press, Nedlands.

Altman, J. C. (Chairman) 1989, *The Aboriginal Arts and Crafts Industry*, Report of the Review Committee, AGPS, Canberra.

Altman, J. C. 1999, 'Aboriginal art centres and NACISS: an appraisal of performance based on financial statements', in F. Wright and F. Morphy (eds), *The Art and Craft Centre Story*, vol. 2, *Summary and Recommendations*, ATSIC, Canberra.

—— 2000, 'The economic status of Indigenous Australians', *CAEPR Discussion Paper No. 193*, CAEPR, ANU, Canberra.

—— 2002, 'Sustainable development options on Aboriginal land: the hybrid economy in the twenty-first century', *CAEPR Discussion Paper No. 226*, CAEPR, ANU, Canberra.

—— 2003, *An Indigenous Arts Strategy for the Northern Territory: Recommended Framework*, Report to Northern Territory Department of Community Development, Sport and Cultural Affairs, Darwin.

—— and Allen, L. M. 1992, 'Indigenous participation in the informal economy: Statistical and policy implications', in J. C. Altman (ed.), *A National Survey of Indigenous Australians: Options and Implications*, CAEPR Research Monograph No. 3, CAEPR, ANU, Canberra.

—— and Taylor, L. 1989, *The Economic Viability of Aboriginal Outstations and Homelands*, AGPS, Canberra.

Australian Bureau of Statistics (ABS) 1996a, *1994 National Aboriginal and Torres Strait Islander Survey: Jabiru ATSIC Region*, cat. no. 4196.0.00.031, ABS, Canberra.

—— 1996b. 'When ERPs aren't enough: a discussion of issues associated with service population estimation', *Demography Working Paper 96/4*, ABS, Canberra.

—— 1998, *Australian Indigenous Geographical Classification 1996*, cat. no. 4706.0.30.001, ABS, Canberra.

—— 1999, 'Service population study: an investigation to assess the feasibility of producing service population estimates for selected LGAs', *Demography Working Paper 99/3*, ABS, Canberra.

—— 2002a, *Deaths 2001*, cat. no. 3302.0, ABS, Canberra.

—— 2002b, *Housing and Infrastructure in Aboriginal and Torres Strait Islander Communities 2001, Australia*, cat. no. 4710.0, ABS, Canberra.

—— 2003, *Criminal Courts*, cat. no. 4513.0, ABS, Canberra.

—— and Australian Institute of Health and Welfare (AIHW) 2003, *The Health and Welfare of Australia's Aboriginal and Torres Strait Islander Peoples 2003*, cat. no. 4704.0, ABS, Canberra.

—— and Centre for Aboriginal Economic Policy Research (CAEPR) 1996, *1994 National Aboriginal and Torres Strait Islander Survey: Employment Outcomes for Indigenous Australians*, cat. no. 4199.0, ABS, Canberra.

—— and National Centre for Epidemiology and Population Health (NCEPH) 1997, *Occasional Paper: Self Assessed Health Status, Indigenous Australians 1994*, cat. no. 4707.0, ABS, Canberra.

Balchin, P., Sykora, L. and Bull, G. 1999, *Regional Policy and Planning in Europe*, Routledge, London.

Bartlett, B., Duncan, P., Alexander, D. and Hardwick, J. 1997, *Central Australian Health Planning Study Final Report*, PlanHealth Pty Ltd, Coledale, NSW.

Bartlett, B. and Duncan, P. 2000, *Top End Aboriginal Health Planning Study*, Report to the Top End Regional Indigenous Health Planning Committee of the Northern Territory Aboriginal Health Forum, PlanHealth Pty Ltd, Coledale, NSW.

Beck, E. J. 1985, *The Enigma of Aboriginal Health*, AIAS, Canberra.

Bell, M. 1992, *Demographic Projections and Forecasts in Australia: A Directory and Digest*, AGPS, Canberra.

Biles, D. 1983, *Groote Eylandt Prisoners: A Research Report*, Australian Institute of Criminology, Canberra.

Binka, F., Ngom, P., Phillips, J. F., Adazu, K. F., & MacLeod, B. B. 1999, 'Assessing population dynamics in a rural African society: the Navrongo demographic surveillance system', *Journal of Biosocial Science*, 31:375–91.

Birckhead, J. 1999, 'Brief encounters: doing rapid ethnography in Aboriginal Australia', in S. Toussaint and J. Taylor (eds), *Applied Anthropology in Australasia*, University of Western Australia Press, Perth.

Brady, M., Kunitz, S. J. and Nash, D. 1997, 'Who's definition? Australian Aborigines, conceptualisations of health and the World Health Organisation', in M. Worboys and L. Marks (eds), *Ethnicity and Health: Historical and Contemporary Perspectives*, Routledge, London.

Commonwealth of Australia 1999, *The National Indigenous Housing Guide: Improving the Living Environment for Safety, Health and Sustainability*, Commonwealth, State and Territory Housing Ministers' Working Group on Indigenous Housing, Canberra.

—— 2003, *Report on Government Services 2003*, vol. 1, *Education Justice, Emergency Management*, Productivity Commission, Melbourne.

Cunningham, J. 1998, 'Implications of changing Indigenous population estimates for monitoring health trends', *Australasian Epidemiologist*, 5 (1): 6–8.

Davis, S. and Prescott, J. R. W. 1992, *Aboriginal Frontiers and Boundaries in Australia*, Melbourne University Press, Melbourne.

Desmarchelier, X. 2001, A Historical and Cultural Overview to the Re-emergence of Thamarrurr: A Traditional Form of Governance for the People of Wadeye, MA Thesis in Aboriginal Affairs Administration, University of South Australia, Adelaide.

Divarakan-Brown, C. 1985, 'Premature ageing in the Aboriginal community', *Proceedings of the Annual Conference of the Australian Association of Gerontology*, 20: 33–4.

Dodson, M. and Smith, D. E. 2003, 'Good governance for sustainable development: strategic issues and principles for Indigenous Australian communities', *CAEPR Discussion Paper No. 250*, CAEPR, ANU, Canberra.

Earle, R. and Earle, L. D. 1999, 'Male Indigenous and non-Indigenous ageing: a new millennium community development challenge', *South Pacific Journal of Psychology*, 11 (2): 13–23.

Falkenberg, J. 1962, *Kin and Totem: Group Relations of Australian Aborigines in the Port Keats District*, Humanities Press, New York.

Falkenberg, A. and Falkenberg J. 1981, *The Affinal Relationship System: A New Approach to Kinship and Marriage among the Australian Aborigines at Port Keats*, Universitetsforlaget, Oslo.

Freeman, T. W. 1961, *A Hundred Years of Geography*, Gerald Duckworth, London.

Glasson, J. 1983, *An Introduction to Regional Planning*, Hutchinson, London.

Gore, C. 1984, *Regions in Question: Space, Development Theory and Regional Policy*, Methuen, London.

Gray, A. 1983, 'Aboriginal fertility at the time of European contact: the Daly River Mission baptismal register', *Aboriginal History*, 7 (1): 80–90.

—— 1989, 'Aboriginal migration to the cities', *Journal of the Australian Population Association*, 6 (2): 122–44.

Hartshorne, R. 1939, *The Nature of Geography*, Association of American Geographers, Lancaster, PA.

Holman, C. D. J. et al. 1990, *The Quantification of Drug-Caused Mortality and Morbidity in Australia, 1988*, DCSH, Canberra.

Howitt, R. 1993, 'Social Impact Assessment as applied peoples' geography', *Australian Geographical Studies*, 31 (2): 127–40.

Hunter, B. H. 1996, 'The determinants of Aboriginal employment outcomes: the importance of education and training', *CAEPR Discussion Paper No. 115*, CAEPR, ANU, Canberra.

—— and Borland, J. 1999, 'The effect of arrest on Aboriginal employment prospects', *Crime and Justice Bulletin No. 45*, NSW Bureau of Crime Statistics and Research, Attorney General's Department, Sydney.

—— and Daly, A. E. 1998, 'Labour market incentives among Aboriginal Australians: the cost of job loss versus the gains from employment', *CAEPR Discussion Paper No. 159*, CAEPR, ANU, Canberra.

International Development Research Centre (IDRC) 2002, *Population and Health in Developing Countries: Volume 1 Population, Health, and Survival at INDEPTH Sites*, IDRC Ottawa.

Ivory, B. 2003, Nemarluk to Heavy Metal: Cultural Change and the Development of Contemporary Youth Sub-culture at Port Keats, Northern Territory, BA Honours thesis, Charles Darwin University, Darwin.

Jones, R. 1994, *The Housing Need of Indigenous Australians, 1991*, CAEPR Research Monograph No. 8, CAEPR, ANU, Canberra.

Josif, P. and Associates 1995a, *The Yugul Mangi Environmental Health Action Plan 1994/95–1998/99*, Yugul Mangi Community Government Council, Ngukurr.

—— 1995b, *Yugul Mangi Housing Action Plan 1994/95–1998/99 Part One*, NT Department of Lands, Housing and Local Government, Darwin.

—— 1995c, *Yugul Mangi Housing Action Plan 1994/95–1998/99 Part Two*, NT Department of Lands, Housing and Local Government, Darwin.

Kardu Numida Incorporated 2002, 'Submission to the Commonwealth Inquiry into Capacity Building in Indigenous Communities, August 2002', House of Representatives Standing Committee on Aboriginal and Torres Strait Islander Affairs, Parliament House, Canberra.

Kinfu, Y. and Taylor, J. 2002, 'Estimating the components of Indigenous population change, 1996–2001', *CAEPR Discussion Paper No. 243*, CAEPR, ANU, Canberra.

Lester, I. A. 1994, *Australia's Food and Nutrition*, AGPS, Canberra.

Long, J. P. M. 1961, Port Keats Population, unpublished report to the Northern Territory Administration Welfare Branch, Darwin (held at AIATSIS, Canberra).

Martin, D. 2002, 'Counting the Wik: the 2001 Census in Aurukun, western Cape York Peninsula', in D. Martin, F. Morphy, W. Sanders, J. Taylor, *Making Sense of the Census: Observations of the 2001 Enumeration in Remote Aboriginal Australia*, CAEPR Research Monograph No. 22, CAEPR, ANU, Canberra.

Martin, D. and Taylor, J. 1996, 'Ethnographic perspectives on the enumeration of Aboriginal people in remote Australia', *Journal of the Australian Population Association*, 13 (1): 17–33.

McCrone, G. 1969, *Regional Policy in Britain*, George Allen and Unwin, London.

Memmott, P. and Meltzer, A. 2003, 'Social capital in Aboriginal Australia: a case study in Wadeye, Northern Territory', paper presented at the *Australian Anthropological Society Annual Conference*, 1–3 October 2003, Camperdown campus, University of Sydney.

Morphy, F. 2002, 'When systems collide: the 2001 Census at a Northern Territory outstation', in D. Martin, F. Morphy, W. Sanders, J. Taylor, *Making Sense of the Census: Observations of the 2001 Enumeration in Remote Aboriginal Australia*, CAEPR Research Monograph No. 22, CAEPR, ANU, Canberra.

Morphy, H. 1999, 'The Reeves Report and the idea of the "region"', In J. C. Altman, F. Morphy and T. Rowse (eds), *Land Rights at Risk? Evaluations of the Reeves Report*, CAEPR Research Monograph No. 14, CAEPR, ANU, Canberra.

Natoli, M. 1982, 'Cultural influences on birth practices in Northern Australia amongst Aboriginals', *Australasian Nurses Journal*, 11 (5): 12–13.

Northern Territory Department of Health and Community Services (NTDHCS) 2003, *The Chronicle*, August/September, 2003.

Northern Territory Department of Education (NTDE) 1999, *Learning Lessons: An Independent Review of Indigenous Education in the Northern Territory*, Government Printing Office of the Northern Territory, Darwin.

Northern Territory Government 2001, *Environmental Health Standards for Remote Communities in the Northern Territory*, Territory Housing, Department of Local Government, Darwin.

Northern Territory Government 2003a, 'Building effective Indigenous governance: the way forward for Northern Territory regions and communities', Summary Paper for the *Building Effective Indigenous Governance* Conference, Jabiru, 4–7 November, 2003, viewed 2003 www.governanceconference.nt.gov.au

—— 2003b, *Building Strong Arts Business: Northern Territory Indigenous Arts Strategy*, Northern Territory Department of Community Development, Sport and Cultural Affairs, Darwin.

—— 2003c, *Building Stronger Regions, Stronger Futures*, Northern Territory Department of Community Development, Sport and Cultural Affairs, Darwin.

Ogilvie, E. and Van Zyl, A. 2001, 'Young Indigenous males, custody and the rites of passage', *Trends and Issues in Crime and Criminal Justice No. 204*, Australian Institute of Criminology, Canberra.

Peterson, N. 1976, 'The natural and cultural areas of Aboriginal Australia', in N. Peterson (ed.), *Tribes and Boundaries in Australia*, Social Anthropology Series No. 10, AIAS, Canberra.

Pholeros, P., Rainow, S. and Torzillo, P. 1993, *Housing for Health: Towards a Healthy Living Environment for Aboriginal Australia*, Health Habitat, Newport Beach, NSW.

Pye, J. 1973, *The Port Keats Story*, J. R. Coleman, Printer, Darwin.

Reeves, J. 1998, *Building on Land Rights for the Next Generation: Report of the Review of the Aboriginal Land Rights (Northern Territory) Act 1976* [2 volumes], AGPS, Canberra.

Reynolds, M. 1994, 'Educational Transition in a Remote Aboriginal Community: Aboriginal-isation in Our Lady of the Sacred Heart School, Wadeye', BA Honours thesis, Monash University, Melbourne.

Rowley C. D. 1971a, *Outcasts in White Australia*, ANU Press, Canberra.

—— 1971b, *The Remote Aborigines*, ANU Press, Canberra.

Sanders, W. 2002, 'Adapting to circumstance: the 2001 Census in the Alice Springs town camps', in D. Martin, F. Morphy, W. Sanders and J. Taylor, *Making Sense of the Census: Observations of the 2001 Enumeration in Remote Aboriginal Australia*, CAEPR Research Monograph No. 22, CAEPR, ANU, Canberra.

—— 2004, 'Prospects for regionalism in Indigenous community governance', paper presented at AIATSIS, 27 April 2004.

Schwab, R. G. 1995, 'The calculus of reciprocity: principles and implications of Aboriginal sharing', *CAEPR Discussion Paper No. 100*, CAEPR, ANU, Canberra.

—— 1998, 'Educational "failure" and educational "success" in an Aboriginal community', *CAEPR Discussion Paper No. 161*, CAEPR, ANU, Canberra.

Senior, K. A. 2003, A Gudbala Laif?: Health and Well-being in a Remote Aboriginal Community: What are the Problems and Where Lies Responsibility? PhD thesis, ANU, Canberra.

Smith, D. E. 1991, 'Toward an Aboriginal household expenditure survey: conceptual, methodological and cultural considerations', *CAEPR Discussion Paper No. 10*, CAEPR, ANU, Canberra.

—— 1996, 'From cultural diversity to regionalism: the political culture of difference in ATSIC', in P. Sullivan (ed.), *Shooting the Banker: Essays on ATSIC and Self-Determination*, NARU, ANU, Darwin.

—— 2000, *Indigenous Families and the Welfare System: Two Community Case Studies*, CAEPR Research Monograph no. 17, CAEPR, ANU, Canberra.

—— 2004 (forthcoming), 'Regionalising governance: policy challenges in the implementation of Regional Authorities in the Northern Territory', *CAEPR Discussion Paper*, CAEPR, ANU, Canberra

Stanley, O. 1985, *The Mission and Peppimenarti: An Economic Study of Two Daly River Aboriginal Communities*, NARU, ANU, Darwin.

Stanner, W. E. H. 1933, 'The Daly River tribes: a report of fieldwork in North Australia', *Oceania*, 3 (4): 377–405.

—— 1933–34, 'Ceremonial economics of the Mulluk Mulluk and Madngella tribes of the Daly River, North Australia: a preliminary paper', *Oceania*, 4: 156–75.

—— 1936a, 'Aboriginal modes of address and reference in the north-west of the Northern Territory', *Oceania*, 7 (4): 301–15.

—— 1936b, 'Murinbata kinship and totemism', *Oceania*, 7 (4): 186–216.

Stilwell, F. 1992, *Understanding Cities and Regions: Spatial Political Economy*, Pluto Press, Leichardt, NSW.

Stohr, W. B. and Fraser Taylor, D. R. 1981, *Development from Above or Below? The Dialectics of Regional Planning In Developing Countries*, John Wiley and Sons, Chichester.

Sutton, P. 1995, *Country: Aboriginal Boundaries and Land Ownership In Australia*, Aboriginal History Monograph No. 3, Aboriginal History Inc., Canberra.

Taylor, J. 1992, 'Geographic location and economic status: a census-based analysis of outstations in the Northern Territory', *Australian Geographical Studies*, 30 (2): 163–84.

—— 1998, 'Measuring short-term population mobility among Aboriginal Australians: options and implications', *Australian Geographer*, 29 (1): 125–37.

—— 1999, 'Aboriginal people in the Kakadu region: social indicators for impact assessment', *CAEPR Working Paper No. 4*, CAEPR, ANU, Canberra.

—— 2002, 'The spatial context of Indigenous service delivery', *CAEPR Working Paper No. 16*, CAEPR, ANU, Canberra.

—— 2003, 'Indigenous Australians: the first transformation', in S. E. Khoo and P. McDonald (eds), *The Transformation of Australia's Population: 1970–2030*, UNSW Press, Sydney.

—— 2004, *Aboriginal Population Profiles for Development Planning in the Northern East Kimberley*, CAEPR Research Monograph No. 23, ANU E Press, Canberra.

—— and Bell, M. 2002, 'The Indigenous population of Cape York Peninsula, 2001–2016', *CAEPR Discussion Paper No. 227*, CAEPR, ANU, Canberra.

—— and —— 2004, 'Continuity and change in Indigenous Australian population mobility', in J. Taylor and M. Bell (eds), *Population Mobility and Indigenous Peoples in Australasia and North America*, Routledge, London.

—— Bern, J. and Senior, K. A. 2000, *Ngukurr at the Millenium: A Baseline Profile for Social Impact Planning in South East Arnhem Land*, CAEPR Research Monograph No. 17, CAEPR, ANU, Canberra.

—— and Biddle, N. 2004, The Relative Socioeconomic Status of Indigenous People in the Murray–Darling Basin, Report to the Murray–Darling Basin Commission Indigenous Action Plan, CAEPR, ANU, Canberra.

—— and Westbury, N. 2000, *Aboriginal Nutrition and the Nyirranggulung Health Strategy in Jawoyn Country*, CAEPR Research Monograph No. 19, CAEPR, ANU, Canberra.

Thamarrurr Rangers 2003, *Thamarrurr Region Land and Sea Management Plan, Part 1*, Thamarrurr Rangers, Wadeye, NT.

Unwin, E., Codde, J., Swensen, G. and Saunders, P. 1997, *Alcohol-Caused Deaths and Hospitalisation in Western Australia by Health Services*, Health Department Western Australia and WA Drug Abuse Strategy Office, Perth.

Walsh, F. and Mitchell, P. 2002, *Planning for Country: Cross-Cultural Approaches to Decision-Making on Aboriginal Lands*, IAD Press, Alice Springs, NT.

Walsh, M. 1989, *The Wagaitj in Relation to the Kenbi Land Claim*, NLC, Darwin.

—— 1990, Language Socialization at Wadeye, unpublished ms, AIATSIS Collections (MS 3555), AIATSIS, Canberra.

Ward, T. 1983, *The Peoples and their Land around Wadeye: Murrinh Kanhi-Ka Kardu I Da Ngarra Putek Pigunu*, Wadeye Press, Wadeye, NT.

Warner, W. L. 1937, *A Black Civilization: A Social Study of an Australian Tribe*, Harper & Brothers, New York.

Willis, J. 1995, 'Fatal attraction: do high technology treatments for end stage renal disease benefit Aboriginal people in central Australia?' *Australian and New Zealand Journal of Public Health*, 19 (6): 603–9.

Wright, F. 1999. *The Art and Craft Centre Story*, vol. 1, *Report*, ATSIC, Canberra.

CAEPR Research Monograph Series

1. *Aborigines in the Economy: A Select Annotated Bibliography of Policy-Relevant Research 1985–90*, L.M. Allen, J.C. Altman, and E. Owen (with assistance from W.S. Arthur), 1991.

2. *Aboriginal Employment Equity by the Year 2000*, J.C. Altman (ed.), published for the Academy of Social Sciences in Australia, 1991.

3. *A National Survey of Indigenous Australians: Options and Implications*, J.C. Altman (ed.), 1992.

4. *Indigenous Australians in the Economy: Abstracts of Research, 1991–92*, L.M. Roach and K.A. Probst, 1993.

5. *The Relative Economic Status of Indigenous Australians, 1986–91*, J. Taylor, 1993.

6. *Regional Change in the Economic Status of Indigenous Australians, 1986–91*, J. Taylor, 1993.

7. *Mabo and Native Title: Origins and Institutional Implications*, W. Sanders (ed.), 1994.

8. *The Housing Need of Indigenous Australians, 1991*, R. Jones, 1994.

9. *Indigenous Australians in the Economy: Abstracts of Research, 1993–94*, L.M. Roach and H.J. Bek, 1995.

10. *The Native Title Era: Emerging Issues for Research, Policy, and Practice*, J. Finlayson and D.E. Smith (eds), 1995.

11. *The 1994 National Aboriginal and Torres Strait Islander Survey: Findings and Future Prospects*, J.C. Altman and J. Taylor (eds), 1996.

12. *Fighting Over Country: Anthropological Perspectives*, D.E. Smith and J. Finlayson (eds), 1997.

13. *Connections in Native Title: Genealogies, Kinship, and Groups*, J.D. Finlayson, B. Rigsby, and H.J. Bek (eds), 1999.

14. *Land Rights at Risk? Evaluations of the Reeves Report*, J.C. Altman, F. Morphy, and T. Rowse (eds), 1999.

15. *Unemployment Payments, the Activity Test, and Indigenous Australians: Understanding Breach Rates*, W. Sanders, 1999.

16. *Why Only One in Three? The Complex Reasons for Low Indigenous School Retention*, R.G. Schwab, 1999.

17. *Indigenous Families and the Welfare System: Two Community Case Studies*, D.E. Smith (ed.), 2000.

18. *Ngukurr at the Millennium: A Baseline Profile for Social Impact Planning in South-East Arnhem Land*, J. Taylor, J. Bern, and K.A. Senior, 2000.

19. *Aboriginal Nutrition and the Nyirranggulung Health Strategy in Jawoyn Country*, J. Taylor and N. Westbury, 2000.

20. *The Indigenous Welfare Economy and the CDEP Scheme*, F. Morphy and W. Sanders (eds), 2001.

21. *Health Expenditure, Income and Health Status among Indigenous and Other Australians*, M.C. Gray, B.H. Hunter, and J. Taylor, 2002.

22. *Making Sense of the Census: Observations of the 2001 Enumeration in Remote Aboriginal Australia*, D.F. Martin, F. Morphy, W.G. Sanders and J. Taylor, 2002.

23. *Aboriginal Population Profiles for Development Planning in the Northern East Kimberley* J. Taylor, 2003.

For information on CAEPR Discussion Papers, Working Papers and Research Monographs please contact:

Publication Sales, Centre for Aboriginal Economic Policy Research,
The Australian National University, Canberra, ACT, 0200

Telephone: 02–6125 8211
Facsimile: 02–6125 2789

Information on CAEPR abstracts and summaries of all CAEPR print publications and those published electronically can be found at the following WWW address:

http://www.anu.edu.au/caepr/

www.ingramcontent.com/pod-product-compliance
Lightning Source LLC
Chambersburg PA
CBHW061228270326
41928CB00025B/3449